WILL THE *REAL* BOSS PLEASE STAND UP?

WILL THE *REAL* BOSS PLEASE STAND UP?

TAKING YOUR ADMINISTRATIVE CAREER TO THE NEXT LEVEL

GEORGE-ANNE FAY

AMERICAN MANAGEMENT ASSOCIATION

NEW YORK • ATLANTA • BOSTON • CHICAGO • KANSAS CITY • SAN FRANCISCO • WASHINGTON, D.C.
BRUSSELS • MEXICO CITY • TOKYO • TORONTO

*This publication is designed to provide accurate and authoritative
information in regard to the subject matter covered. It is sold with
the understanding that the publisher is not engaged in rendering
legal, accounting, or other professional service. If legal advice or
other expert assistance is required, the services of a competent
professional person should be sought.*

Library of Congress Cataloging-in-Publication Data

Fay, George-Anne.
   *Will the real boss please stand up? : taking your administrative
career to the next level / George-Anne Fay.*
      p.   cm.
   Includes index.
   ISBN 0-8144-0422-7
   1. Secretaries—Vocational guidance.   I. Title.
HF5547.5.F39   1998
651.3'741'02373—dc21   *98-5647*
                                                                  CIP

Printing number

10   9   8   7   6   5   4   3   2   1

TABLE OF CONTENTS

In honor of Anne C. Fay

Theresa Nauss for all the laughs

Kimberly Smith, without whom Fay Associates, Inc.,
would not have grown

Andrea Scott, for unfailing support

Caitie Fay, whose future lies ahead

National Speakers Association, for encouraging me
to speak my heart

Ellen Kadin, who believed in my work

Andrea Iadanza, Jackie Green, and Ann O'Connor,
who keep the message alive in my programs

Elinor Basso, who believed in program support for
this important audience

Marie Stamos, who always knows the right word

Peter, Judy, Barbara, Ann, Joanie, Julie, Tim, and
Victor at AMA in Washington, D.C., a
magnificent team of professionals
and especially,
Alan, my loving husband, who shares life's
excitement and possibilities with me every day

David, Rick, and Scott Pittaway for their support of
us both

FOREWORD

When I graduated from college with a bachelor's degree in journalism, I knew I wasn't cut out for the daily grind of newspaper work. But I was clueless about what to do and where to go with my education. My skills were limited to a) typing and b) the ability to spell "accommodation" and "liaison" correctly.

So I became a girl friday for a public relations firm in Manhattan, and then a receptionist.

But, in truth, I was certainly unqualified for any kind of office professional position. Even though my spelling was good and my typing accurate, my organizational skills were terrible. My rate of productivity was even worse. I had a towering in-box that eventually turned into three stacks of typing that needed to be done, and my attitude was inexcusable. As a college graduate, I thought I was too good for the job. But, in reality, I was just a young pipsqueak with no office experience. The job was, in fact, too good for me.

That was twenty years ago. Now when I look back on my Manhattan days, I'm grateful for the experience. And I see those early jobs as my first steps into a world of possibilities, adventure, and self-discovery. As the years have flown, I've come to recognize that all work is packed with the potential for growth, fulfillment, and self-expression. But in those days, we just didn't talk about work like that. We certainly didn't find books about it on the shelves.

If I had had a book like this to read back then, I would have been much smarter about how I approached the privilege of being of service to a great man and a great cause.

Being of service . . . that's a calling every office professional can be proud of. This book is the first one I've seen that gets to the heart of what it really means to bring dignity, self-respect, pride, and control to the job of being an office professional.

You have a noble calling . . . and a powerful one. It is packed with many opportunities to make a real difference in the world and in your own personal circumstances. As you turn the pages, you'll see what I mean.

Martha Finney, co-author
Find Your Calling, Love Your Life

1

GOT A SEC?

I am very happy to be able to start this book with some excellent news: Hollywood finally understands how important office professionals really are to happy endings. What? Am I out of my mind? Hollywood? Recent shows are running through your head right now. I know, I can see them playing in your mind's eye. *Working Girl* (not exactly complimentary to ambitious support professionals); *The Temp* (pretty scary stuff coming from someone who was only on the job for a few hours). And then there is *Murphy Brown* and her succession of nightmare secretaries, or the frantic, distracted go-fer on *Mad About You*, or the absolutely bizarre temporary who vies for Matthew's coveted spot as the Office Weird Guy on *News Radio*.

All right. So maybe it's not a 100 percent hopeful situation. But let me tell you about two movies that came out the same year I was writing this book: *The Associate* and *Air Force One*. In both movies (one a light, situation comedy and the other an action-packed adventure), a secretary saves the day and turns the course of the story in favor of the hero. (Now that I've written that, I'm thinking maybe the secretary was the hero.)

In *The Associate*, Dianne Wiest tries to persuade new entrepreneur Whoopi Goldberg to hire her as an assistant. "No can do," says Whoopi. "I'm struggling so much I can't even get on Mr. Big's calendar! Without him as a client, I'm going under."

"No problem," says Dianne. She picks up the phone, punches in Mr. Big's number, chats up Mr. Big's assistant, and treats the assistant kindly and courteously, while expressing sincere, personal interest in her life and concerns. Without skipping a beat, Dianne says, "Say, there's someone I think Mr. Big should meet. Would you mind putting her on his calendar?" Snip snap, it's done. And the next thing we know, Whoopi is out of her bunny slippers and wearing a drop-dead gorgeous red silk outfit at a fancy ball.

In *Air Force One*, things start out as per usual. The President of the United States is much admired and very busy. So busy, in fact, that he simply signs the papers thrust under his nose by his cheerful, smiling assistant. Only after the ink is already on the paper does he ask what he has just signed. "Nothing to worry about," she says, walking away, her mind already on her next task. It's clear from the "Yeah, she's probably right" shrug of his shoulders that the President has all the confidence in the world in her.

An hour into the movie, the President and his plane, including all those aboard, are doomed. The only chance they have to save themselves is to somehow get a fax to the White House. "But we can't!" says a highly ranked in-flight executive, who reminds the President that the bad guys cut the phone lines and, therefore, the fax line must be dead, too. "Oh, rats," says the President.

Who steps up and saves the day? The office assistant. She respectfully informs the President that the fax lines and the phone lines were wired differently into the plane. Therefore, the fax lines are probably intact. How does she know this? Probably because she has used those fax machines daily on routine jobs. Maybe she was also the one to requisition service repair on the onboard fax and phones. Maybe she's in charge of the entire office support infrastructure on board Air Force One.

All of those things are possible, even plausible. The federal government has suffered as much downsizing as any private corporation has over the last fifteen years. So maybe this fictitious character found herself in charge of the whole plane because the middle management structure had disappeared.

The plane is saved—at least for a little while. And the secretary ultimately gets a safe parachute ride out of the back hatch, grinning with the adventure of it all as she jumps.

It could happen. I know because I see last-minute saves happen every day. At no other time in history have office professionals had the opportunity they do now to step up to the plate, expand their circles of contacts, achieve respect up and down any organization chart, and take on new challenges and new projects. And even save the day now and then. It's all in a day's work, right?

I'm calling this first chapter "Got a Sec?" for a reason. I know how busy you are. And I know how often you're interrupted every day. And I know that rarely is anyone courteous enough to ask you, "Got a sec?" It's usually "Drop what you're doing and do this instead. It won't take more than a sec."

And I know that even a second here and there is a rare commodity for professionals like you. So, I designed this book in short chapters so you can read it in just a second here and there. And I hope it's the very last book you'll ever read about being an office professional. From now on, your reading list should be the same reading list as your supervisors' and *their* supervisors'. (In fact, find out what the CEO is reading, and read that.)

Don't expect any discussions on grammar in this book or instructions on how to spell "accommodate" and "liaison." If you're advanced enough in your career and ambition to be reading this kind of book, you certainly know how to look those things up.

I'm here to help you look at your career in a new way. To help you reevaluate some of the little things you do or cope with during the workday. And then help you reposition yourself and your role in the organization to best take advantage of all the experience you've accumulated already—and to prepare yourself for an even better and more profitable career.

My purpose is to be your no-pressure or low-pressure companion as you leisurely consider the many different ways you can capitalize on the strengths, skills, and goals that you have already. By the time you finish this book my hope is that you will have the added confidence and sense of purpose that will position you for an even more promising career and an even more rewarding paycheck.

To make this book more fun to read—it certainly made it more fun to write—I am including an exciting collection of profiles about special experts in the office profession, experts who are just like you. I have discovered over my years of training that talking with hands-on professionals is the best way to keep up with the trends and wisdom that are developing in this dynamic career. I'm so grateful that they took the time out of their busy days and schedules to share their stories, straight from the heart. I hope that perhaps you will see yourself in their stories and insights. I also hope that they will inspire you to think about some of the wisdom that *you* have collected so far in your career . . . and pass it on to the ones coming up behind you.

But first I'd like to tell you a little bit about myself, a little more about what it means to be an office professional today, and then go into some discussion about why you work. No, it's not entirely for the money. Surprised?

So, turn the page and let's get acquainted. That is, if you have a sec.

2

DAD WASN'T ALWAYS RIGHT

I think an important milestone in our individual stories of growing up is the moment we hear our father spout some wisdom but then surprise ourself with our own opinion. We discover for the first time that he's talking out of his hat!

For me it happened the day my father and I drove downtown together. He was going to work, and I was going to school. "Remember, George-Anne," he said, "you don't always have to be first."

Well, I didn't know why not. Someone had to be first. It might as well be me, I reasoned. I didn't know it then, but that was my first lesson in positioning. Did that mean I was pushy and stepped on other people's toes? Maybe it did, now and then. But mostly it didn't. I was just this fiery, red-haired ball of ambition happy to walk through any door that would open for me. That tendency revealed itself early. I was an entrepreneur before I was even out of grammar school, selling chocolate bars to all my uncles who lived at home after returning from the Korean War. They were students themselves in those days, catching up on their lost college years by day and their social lives at night. Those boys needed their energy! I saw a need and I filled it—at a profit.

The payoff certainly didn't make me the chocolate mogul of my neighborhood, but it did give me the sweet taste of being rewarded for spotting an opportunity. So it came as no surprise to anyone that this eager little girl would one day grow up to major in business in college.

The first big city job I landed was in the personnel department of Filene's in Boston. Personnel, in those days, did not have the organizational respect its modern cousin, human resources management, has today.

That first job began a three-decade journey of personal and professional growth. I know many people think those are two separate paths, but I've never been able to separate the two. Success at work fuels personal confidence, which then boosts energy for making an even bigger difference on the job. Growth comes from every experience in life, and I could not have developed personally were it not for my business successes.

That first job at Filene's strapped me onto my own personal booster rocket. Sure, there were some sputters and spits—with more than enough smoke—on the way up. But it's always been up for me.

After becoming bored with retail, I thought it would be fun to move to New York City and try the Wall Street life. With each new city, I became more and more alive. I was excited by the different pulses that each city offered, by the new business cultures that opened up to me, and by the people I met in places ranging from boardrooms to rugby fields in Central Park.

You've probably heard this key-to-success nugget of wisdom: that the way to succeed is to volunteer for those jobs that no one else wants to do. That's what I did, and before long I was queen of my own little kingdom at the brokerage house where I worked. My little nation was known as "branch management," and I got it all: personnel, supplies, the mail room, training. If it happened today, I probably would have also found a way to snap up information management systems.

For me, Wall Street was the hands-on version of the Harvard Business School; it was the ultimate on-the-job-training. Its fast pace energized me. In fact, I would run three miles a day with the company's brokers along East River Drive—just to learn from them the nuances of the trader's desk and the real decision-making techniques. While most of the women I knew and worked with were being tutored by mentors who assigned them tasks, I was seeking and finding sponsors, who opened doors for me.

I learned lessons that would serve me well throughout the following years, lessons I'll describe as we move through this book together. Eventually one special door opened for me—the door of romance—and as I walked through it, I found myself one of the many thousands of transplants who cycle in and out of the Washington, D.C., area every year.

The romance failed, but I flourished. Taking on each new challenge as it crossed my path, I was able to capitalize on all the support skills I had accumulated along the way. I started a consulting company that provided those same services to downtown firms that were too small to do it all in-house. Yes, my heart felt as if it were breaking for a little while. And yes, I was completely alone and without my precious contacts that I had cultivated so carefully back up in New York. But I was determined to find a place in the D.C. area to throw down roots.

And, yes, I was first. Or very close to it. My little firm was among the first in the nation's capital to meet the ever-increasing demand for outside support assistance that began in the early 1980s and should continue well into the foreseeable future. This little firm of mine helped put the word and practice of outsourcing into the daily contemporary business lexicon. We were the modern pioneers.

Fast forwarding to today, I am happily married to a wonderful man who supports my ambitions. (I consider the departure of my first fiancé to really be an advance wedding gift from him to me and Alan; so I'm thankful for those old memories.) I'm typing away in a little windowed alcove overlooking the scenic Spa Creek in Annapolis, Maryland. The exotic boats floating there come from all over the world and share this little watery acreage with my husband's and my powerboat. And I'm within thirty minutes of one of the world's best airports, which ushers me aboard planes to fly all over the country to share my story.

I don't have to be first anymore. I've grown out of that. *But*

I do have to be there. I have to be anywhere I can show members of the support profession how to position themselves as the most valuable employees any company can have. In this era of downsizing when most executives have no choice but to leave, I want you to be able to stay if you choose, or go if you choose. But go on to better things. That's the ultimate positioning. And that's the result of focused ambition.

3

SURPRISE! DID YOU THINK YOU'D BE AN ASSISTANT?

When I was growing up, most women were still limited in their choice of profession. Sure, there were outstanding female academics, physicians, writers, executives, and scientists. But for most American women who were basically biding their time before marriage and motherhood, the choice was either secretary, teacher, or nurse. For some reason, my family decided that there was only room for one smart daughter in the bunch, and the honor went to my sister, who became a dynamite teacher.

You need school smarts to be a nurse, too, obviously. And my family just couldn't quite imagine me being a reader (wait till they get a load of this book!). So, by default, I was groomed for a life of business.

Well, the irony here is that if there was ever a career that needs a combination of book smarts and street smarts, it is that of office professional. It makes me laugh when I hear career counselors say, "If you want an easy entrée into the work world, start by getting office experience as a secretary."

Sure, that's one way of doing it. But anyone who thinks this career is just an entry-level job or a dead-end position has another "think" coming. Of course, anyone who thinks this way is probably most likely to complain that competent, professional assistants are hard to find. (And even harder to keep, I'd bet.)

But it's also not rocket science. Equip yourself with basic competencies in the most prevalent office software, acquire appropriate communication skills, learn how to construct a professional letter or even write business reports using impeccable spelling and grammar, develop good organizational habits and you have the foundations of a rewarding, relatively stable career. Add to those basics the attitude that life is for learning and you have the beginnings of a career full of surprises and sparkling destinations that you can't even imagine today.

Did you ever think that this is the kind of work that would interest you? Maybe you did. Maybe not. It's often the career that men and women—women, especially—step into after high school or college when nothing else obviously appeals to that person's passion. Now that might sound as if I'm putting down the profession. Quite the contrary: It provides a wonderful world of opportunities to learn, make powerful contacts that you can keep for life, discover new businesses and new careers, and move in high-powered circles.

This is a career that can help you elevate yourself to a new life or simply meet your basic needs while you're waiting for something else to come along . . . or while you're raising a family . . . or while you're earning and saving extra money that you need to make another dream come true.

The role of the office professional, assistant, or secretary can open doors for you. Your job is to pick the best possible doors. No one can tell you which opportunity doors are best for *you*, but there are some fundamental rules of thumb that will lead to your best possible future.

SUCCESS IS SPELLED WITH THREE *E*'S

And those three *e*'s are: *energy, effort,* and *enthusiasm.*

In this book you'll find that I've included interviews with people whom I consider to be successful office professionals. Most of them were surprised to hear from me. After all, when was the last time you read a success profile of someone who was a secretary or administrative assistant? Not recently, I'd bet.

All these people came into the profession from different avenues. Some wanted to work in an office since the time they were tiny children. When others played house, school, or store, they played office. They were born to the job.

Other people found that this work helped them fulfill other priorities. One woman left a high-powered, highly compensated job as a stockbroker because she wanted defined hours. She wanted to be able to leave her work behind her in the evening when she returned home to her children. Others simply grew into the job, without any solid expectations for themselves—only to discover they loved the "in-charge" role they developed for themselves at work.

You might be surprised to see the words "in charge" when you're more often used to seeing the words "of service" when it comes to your kind of work. Who says you can't be both? In fact, I think there is no one more in charge than the person who knows how to get the job done. And to be of service you must know how to get that job done.

But that requires *energy*, *effort*, and *enthusiasm*:

ENERGY

A manager once said to me that his main job was to decide how to spend money. How much energy does *that* take? Especially when you compare his work with yours: How about the constant daylong ups and downs from your desk chair? The gracious smile that covers up your irritation at being interrupted the *umpteenth* time when all you've wanted to do for the last four hours was to get one simple letter printed, signed, and sent. There is a hurry-up-and-wait pace to some of your days, when you just can't get into a rhythm—a *flow*—that would help your day go more smoothly. Soldiers say that warfare can be described as days of bone-tedious boredom marked by a few hours of sheer terror. Does your workday feel that way to you sometimes? That kind of schedule is hard on your system. And it takes energy to somehow rise above the toll it takes on your get-up-and-go.

EFFORT

I knew a surgical nurse once who said that the mark of good operating room assistants is that they know which instrument the surgeon will need long before the surgeon actually needs it. So even as the surgeon's gloved hand extends palm upward to receive the instrument, the assistant already has the correct instrument waiting there. Not a fraction of a second is wasted. But this means the surgical nurse must know *exactly* what the surgeon is doing. And *that* means the surgical nurse must know *exactly* what the surgeon knows. And the two of them work in a mutual groove that saves lives. (Puts a new spin on the expression "hand-in-glove," doesn't it?)

Your work may not be a matter of life and death. But you are working at your best when you are in a similar groove with your supervisors. Do you know what they're doing and why? Can you anticipate what they'll need next week because of the meeting they're having today? Even better, can you anticipate what they'll need next month because of the meeting *another department* is having today?

This kind of career that you have takes effort. Effort in anticipating, in imagining, and in taking your coat off again at the end of the day—just when you are finally ready to go home—to sit back down before your computer to process that newly arrived report that needs an instant turnaround. The effort it takes to sprint across town with a necessary folder or jump into a taxi to rush a forgotten briefcase to the airport before the jet takes off. The effort it takes to creatively develop a give-and-take relationship with your counterparts in other departments so that you can give your supervisor an early heads-up on a new product roll-out, a budget cut, or a policy change.

ENTHUSIASM

Many people sacrifice interest in their work for the sake of either money or "paying their dues" to learn necessary skills.

Writers, for instance, might invest several years in working for a dull newspaper or magazine, just to develop their talent and accumulate samples of their work. They can't always do this in subject areas that are especially interesting to them because the job market for writers is so tight. But the demand for office professionals is so great, you can choose to work in an environment that interests you.

Likewise, you can choose your employer according to your ethics. It's just as easy to find a job with a decent, moral employer as it is to find a job with a company that trespasses on your personal code of right and wrong. Whenever I see examples of these companies on the news or on *60 Minutes,* I always wonder, What were the assistants thinking or doing while all this was going on?

It's hard to be enthusiastic about your work when you know the company is functioning in immoral, illegal, or unethical ways. And you owe it to your own career and work record—indeed, your mental health—to support companies that are doing things right. I tell you more about that in Chapter 10.

Of all the possible careers there are in this world, you have no reason to be either bored or in moral conflict with what you do. I bet you'd never thought you'd see the word "luxury" attached to your career, but yes, it's true. You have the luxury to explore and be very choosy about the kind of work you do and the company you do it for.

Success Is Spelled L-E-A-R-N

By choosing the career of office professional, you are also positioning yourself in a field that will teach you as much as you want as fast as you can absorb it. Companies need professional support staff, and those that are good enough for you will treat you like a rare commodity and do anything and everything necessary to keep you there.

One of the best perks of your position is that you can learn not only the inside details for your company's industry but also how a company works overall—and how the departments work together to achieve the corporation's long-term objectives. For every company function, there is probably at least one assistant assigned to support that activity.

Are you interested in exploring the world of corporate finance? The accounting department is a good place to start learning. Does marketing appeal to you? Then you might want to look for an opening in the public relations, marketing, advertising, or even strategic planning department. Have you been curious about human resources management and how people actually get their jobs? Look for positions in the HR or personnel department. Get a taste of corporate law by working in the legal department. Or perhaps you want to use your international background or language skills. Companies need employees who are willing to travel and live the expatriate life.

Or may you want to watch what happens in the executive suite. Maybe you want to be there when the big decisions are made. Seek out executive assistant positions, and you'll be riding the corporate jet and meeting world-class executives. In these positions you'll experience access and influence that middle management executives only dream of.

The office professional career is also the best possible corporate career path to choose if your ultimate ambition is to start a company of your own one day. Work at a variety of companies to try on different working environments, or find one large company that will enable you to move into a wide selection of divisions. Watch how the departments are run and how they depend on each other. Observe different management styles.

Your career has an advantage that no other profession has. It is the most portable career throughout the entire corporate hierarchy. Watch, observe, ask questions, and listen carefully to the answers. And maybe one day you'll have all the pieces assembled so that you can open your own dream business.

In truth, you already have. You are CEO of Me, Inc. We'll get to that in the next chapter.

4

IN BUSINESS FOR
YOURSELF: ME, INC.

Many phrases are being thrown around in leadership and career management discussions these days. You've probably heard them: "The demise of the employment contract"; "The New Deal"; "No matter who you work for, you're still self-employed"; or "Whatever happened to loyalty to one's employer?"

What does it mean to work for a company in today's environment? And how do you reconcile the need to look out for your own interests and still be loyal to your employer? The key here, which I think no one is really talking about yet, is that there is still corporate loyalty. It has just taken on a different personality.

So I'd like to take this chapter to talk to you about finding the place where your personal career interests and company interests meet. Because this is now a world where people come and go, you might find yourself surrounded by empty desks that had once been occupied by people you knew almost as intimately as your own family. People are still being laid off right and left, even though there is low unemployment and companies are desperate for new talent.

Whether you stay or go should be entirely your choice and within your power to determine. So you'll find ideas later in this book about how to strategize ways to stay, if that is what you want. Or how to strategize ways to position a terrific departure to a new and better future, if that is what you want. In other words, I would like to help you rethink this notion of an uncertain employment world and instead turn it into an idea of expanded opportunities.

This is really a time of unprecedented career security. Now note, I didn't say job security. I said career security. And it all depends on how you look at it. Choose to look at it one way, and you will be a passive victim of someone's misguided attempts to make your company more profitable. And chances will be better that you'll hear, as they say in the summertime, "You're OUT!"

Look at it my way, and you will be the architect of a future that is driven by *your* needs, talents, energy, and choices. Stay at a company if you want. Or leave—if you want. Either way, you'll be loyal to two companies: your employer and Me, Inc. (psst: That's you!).

Now, you might think that your job is as an assistant and, as far as profitable functions are concerned, that's all you are. Wrong! You are your own corporation. Even the word *corporation* reflects your right to consider yourself in those terms. Its root *corp* comes from the Latin *corpus*, which means body. And your body (or life) on earth is also a corporation (Me, Inc.), with its own businesslike departments to support your existence: production, distribution, research and development, marketing, maintenance, and, yes, administration and finance.

So, let's compare Me, Inc., with a type of company that you might be more familiar with—say a fictional corporation that manufactures laundry detergent. Sudso, Inc., produces one product—soap—and does it well. Its customers count on it to wash clothes, but they wouldn't dream of using it for, say, transmission fluid. They know they can count on Sudso to get their clothes clean because it markets itself that way. And they can be relatively sure that Sudso will continually improve its product as its research and development department comes up with new formulas.

Likewise, as a professional assistant, you do your job well. Your customers (your supervisors or team members) know that they can count on you for that task, and they know not to ask you to be a rocket scientist. Because you haven't marketed yourself that way. And your customers hope that your research and development department (that thing between your ears) will continue to keep Me, Inc., current in all your career's developments.

The relationship between Sudso and its customers and the relationship between you and your team members are what the new loyalty (the so-called New Deal) is built on. You, as Me, Inc., expect to be financially compensated for your services—just as Sudso expects to be paid for its boxes of soap. You are loyal to your customers as long as they recognize your value to them and pay you for your product.

Likewise, your customers are loyal to you as long as they can expect the same quality of product or service—if not better—each time they lay their money down. If they don't hold up their end of the bargain, you can sell your product to someone else. You can do this because your marketing department has been busy expanding your sphere of influence—I'll show you how later in this book. And if you don't hold up your end, they can buy the same services from someone else. (In which case, you had better call a corporate meeting, make a fuss, and take names.)

Now there are two more wrinkles I'd like to throw into this pile of laundry: positioning and relationship.

Let's discuss positioning first. We know Sudso makes soap, right? Now Sudso can make soap for low-end customers, for whom value is more important than anything else. It is a good thing that Sudso makes a product to keep everybody's clothes clean. But it still has to be profitable. So it shaves its costs by cutting down on marketing and research and development. Soon, its box isn't as attractive as it used to be, its design is too plain. Research and development is also cut back and the product quickly becomes obsolete. Plenty of other detergents are positioned to take its customer base. Sudso now has to sell a lot of soap just to meet its revenue requirements. That's a lot of hard work.

Or Sudso can *position* itself as the gentle detergent of choice for the finest silks and cashmere. Now we're talking. Sudso can take the same basic formula (provided, of course, that it is indeed high quality and gentle), redesign the box to attract a more sophisticated taste, invest more money in research and development, and increase the price. High-end customers *want* to pay premium prices when they are confident that they're getting premium soap. And by paying that extra price, they're basically paying for the company's research and marketing.

Of course, Sudso might not have as many customers. But then again, with prices like that, Sudso wouldn't have to sell as much soap.

So now my question to you is, How are you positioning Me, Inc.? If you were a soap box, would you be attractively designed? I'm not saying you have to be Ms. or Mr. Universe, but is your packaging at least tidy, bright, and imaginative? Is your marketing message clear, concise, and spelled correctly? Are you marketing yourself to the low-, the mid-, or the high-end market?

Don't get me wrong. Any positioning is respectable and dignified. Honest work for appropriate compensation is respectable. But the higher you position your personal brand of Me, Inc., the more rewarding your work will be, the bigger your personal profit margin, and, in many respects, you won't have to work so darned hard at drudge-level tasks just to keep your personal corporation in the marketplace called Planet Earth.

The last wrinkle, *relationship,* is where your self-interests in Me, Inc., meet with your desire to be loyal to your employer—which is really the Me, Inc., customer. No matter how good and well-priced your product is, relationship is the thing that builds your future profit margins.

Going back to our Sudso example, relationship can also be described as buying habits. For example, I have a friend who buys only Crest toothpaste. Not because it's necessarily any better than Colgate or Gleem or Pepsodent, but because that's the brand her parents bought. And she didn't even have an especially happy childhood! So it's not as if she's linked the taste of Crest with pleasant memories. Her buying habits have simply put her in relationship with Crest. And Sudso's customers' buying habits have put them in relationship with Sudso. That's loyalty.

Who are Me, Inc., customers, and what are their buying habits? Well, naturally, the person you directly report to is a customer. But how about all those people who rely on a productive exchange with your supervisor? They're your customers, too. In fact, the entire company that you work with (as well as its customers, vendors, associates, and even its former employees) is a gigantic collection of customers who are in relationship with you.

Cultivate that relationship up and down the organizational ladders and across functions (the organizational "lattice"), and you will develop an interwoven tapestry of connections and loyalties.

You will be positioned in a double-barreled power center of contacts, excellence, mutual respect, and results. Both corporations will benefit: your employer and Me, Inc.

And then you can name your own price.

───────────── **PROFILE** ─────────────

Betsy Dimarco
Executive Assistant
Waggoner Edstrom
Bellevue, WA

I needed to have a 9 to 5 job that wouldn't bleed over into my family life. So I chose to work for a public relations firm outside Seattle.

I used to be a stockbroker, and once had my own small marketing consulting company. I was also the local counselor for AuPair America. Visa regulations for au pairs require an adult counselor to be within an hour's drive of wherever the au pair is placed. Our job is to help the au pair assimilate into the community, and give him or her someone to turn to other than the host family. AuPair counselors are especially important when emergencies arise, because, of course, the au pairs wouldn't choose standard office hours to have their emergencies. One of my au pairs tried to leap over a bronze pig in Pioneer Square at midnight. She knocked out all her teeth. Another au pair simply disappeared. Turns out she decided to fly home to Norway and drove the family car to the airport without telling anyone.

All these responsibilities started to mount up and become more intrusive on my family life. My two children needed me. So I decided to find a company where I could arrive in the morning, do my job, and be done at the end of the day. I would be totally present when I was there, and totally present at home.

A friend of mine knew about a job like this. I told her, "Oh gosh, I could never do anything like *that.*" I'd always been the person who had assistants reporting to *me.* I didn't think that it would be challenging or rewarding. And I would have to be more demure in my demeanor.

But I was wrong. I assumed I would come into the company knowing the job cold. Instead I had a straight upward learning curve. Part of the challenge was being back in the corporate world. It also took some time to understand how to map my priorities closer to my supervisor's priorities. I really needed to work with him as a team, so we had to quickly get to know each other.

I also relied on the other assistants in the firm. I soon realized that I didn't know this job as well as people who had done it for many years. So I had no problem saying, "Help, I need to rely on your expertise." That helped me win friends. And it was true; I really didn't know the job.

Working here gives me a sense of completion. I really enjoy doing small tasks. Having two small kids at home, nothing ever really gets accomplished. At home there's always a feeling that I should be doing something. At work, I get more of a feeling of accomplishment and I see tangible progress.

I'm also treated with a lot of respect at my job. Servitude would feel like a certain consistent pushing of my limits, a disrespect of my own feelings, and of being taken for granted. But my boss is really good at setting an example for others to follow. It's also a matter of body language. I make sure I meet people's eyes, responding as an adult to them, and responding in a calm manner. When someone is in a flap and needs to get something done, my job is to calmly help that person look at his or her options.

The role of assistant is much more exciting than I thought it would be. I try to assist my supervisor from one decision to another, to help him move forward.

I think success in this kind of relationship depends on picking the right manager to be with from the start, and negotiating up front in the job interview the kind of working relationship you expect. It's not just asking the right questions, but also evaluating the questions that are being asked of you. If your interviewer is only interested in your typing speed or what software packages you know, you can be pretty sure that is all the job will entail. If the interviewer wants to know who you've been and what problems you've solved in the past, you know that the job will call on all your abilities.

People are realizing more and more that support careers are about more than just typing and bringing the coffee. We are actually command central, the glue of the team.

Make no mistake, there is still a hierarchy. But I also have information that is valuable to everyone. Everyone has information, and we become a team when we bring our pieces together. Helping to facilitate the exchange of that information is part of this job.

My advice is:

1. *Determine what success means to you.* For me, success at this stage of my life is getting home on time. But it also means having a job where I'm respected and I'm given the chance to work in a proactive way, taking the initiative wherever I see the chance.

2. *Systemize the routine details of your job.* That way, you can focus on big picture concerns.

3. *Maintain a sense of humor.* For instance, when I'm about to deliver some bad news to my boss, I start singing, "Kiss the day good-bye," from the musical *Chorus Line.* At least we can laugh about the tough luck that's about to come our way. It helps.

5

CHANGE IS GOOD: CONTROL IS BETTER

A friend of mine was flying home to Baltimore from Newark a couple of weeks ago. She sat next to a handsome gentleman with graying temples and a nice smile. A quick glance at the wedding ring on his left hand told her this was going to be a short acquaintance, so she started talking about work. He was an executive with a software company that she recognized as being one that's notoriously difficult on its employees. He's had to fire twenty workers in the last year, he said, all of whom were near retirement. The irony was that the company also had 600 open positions, but none of the former employees were qualified to fill them.

What a shame, they agreed, that the former employees couldn't see the handwriting on the wall and keep their skills current. Then the executive said he had been on some job interviews, and a multinational firm had offered him a salary three times more than his current income to open an office in Baltimore.

"That would mean no more extended travel," he said wistfully. It would mean more time at home with his young children and new baby. But, he said, he was too old now to start anything new. Figuring him to have a much younger wife, my friend passed her eyes over his gray hair and asked him his age. "Thirty-three," he said. Too old to risk a change.

He's too old? He's too old! Here was a classic example of someone being as old as he thinks he is. And while I would never know for sure, I would bet easily that his own desk chair will be empty before long. The big risk he took was deciding to stay where he was.

As much as it saddens me to hear these stories, it also reminds me of the growing power office professionals are gaining as executive desks are cleared out and no one can be found to replace their former occupants. Does that sound like bone-picking? Well, maybe it does. But the opportunities are there. And whether they want to or not, office professionals are being recruited to perform those duties.

So there is good news buried in the terrible circumstance of other people's terminations. As the corporate levels are being flattened, the expression "the new middle manager" has been coined. And, guess what? That's you!

You can forget the title of "secretary." According to a survey conducted in 1997 by the Professional Secretaries International (PSI), it looks like the very word is on its way out. Fewer than half the office professionals surveyed said their title carried that word. The titles "secretary," "executive secretary," and "administrative secretary" are all passé.

In their place are the titles "administrative assistant," "executive assistant," "coordinator," "technician," and "associate." According Gerri Kozlowski, CPS, who was PSI's president for 1997–98, this shift in title largely reflects the expansion of duties in the changing times.

Office professionals must be the key software and information resources in the office, taking on more and more responsibilities as their supervisors and peers depart. In addition to often being the only surviving corporate memory, they're also taking on additional responsibilities, including managing their own projects and correspondence; researching, recommending, and making major purchasing decisions; and training and supervising others.

I would bet that among those 600 openings at that young man's company, there were a healthy number of openings for office support. According to PSI statistics, more than 400,000 new positions are expected to open in the United States alone by the year 2005, making it the tenth fastest growing career in the country! Add computer expertise to your office support skills and you've gained even more job security. You can retire precisely when you want to, not when a prematurely graying young man tells you to push on.

Do you suppose he should consider changing professions? Nope, I guess probably not. The office professional must be one who knows how to blossom in all kinds of economic weather and quickly learn the developing technology. He'd never make the cut.

6

FROM INVISIBLE TO
INVINCIBLE . . . FROM
DISPOSABLE TO
INDISPENSABLE

A few years ago, the Washington office of the American Red Cross underwent a huge change in management. One of the fallouts of the reorganization was that *everyone* had to reapply and reinterview for their jobs—the very jobs some of them have had for years! When I first read about it, I thought it was patently unfair. Here hundreds of employees had done their jobs loyally and faithfully for years, and now they suddenly had to prove again their usefulness to the organization?

But now that the years have passed, and millions of employees have been downsized coast to coast, I realize that the Red Cross was actually just ahead of its time. Daily, whether we're self-employed (as I am now) or seemingly secure in a full-time job, we must renew our contract with our clients and employers. Every evening those contracts expire, only to be renegotiated the next day. We never stop interviewing for our jobs.

In their book *Power Interviews: Job-Winning Tactics from Fortune 500 Recruiters*, authors Neil Yeager and Lee Hough explore different ways executives can position themselves as the lead contenders for openings at some of the country's most important corporations. While most of the book is dedi-

cated to typical questions in today's high-powered employment interviews, it concludes with a compelling list of twelve
corporate trends that drive today's hiring decisions. If you are
able to tell a story of how you've recently dealt with each of
these trends, so the theory goes, you stand a better chance of
rising above the pack of candidates.

If that's the case, the same holds true of incumbents keeping their jobs. And that includes you! So here's the list, and
if you're thinking, "Well, that doesn't affect me, I'm just the
secretary," then think again. And if you really used the word
"just," we'll get to that in a later chapter. But for now, give
some thought to these twelve trends and figure out how you
can use them to position yourself as the most invincible and
indispensable office professional in the organization.

1. *Global competition.* Somewhere on this planet there
is a company based abroad that's positioning itself to eat your
employer's lunch. What are you doing to help position your
company, your department, and your supervisor in the global
marketplace?

2. *Flattening of organizational frameworks.* We've already touched on that in the previous chapter. Now the question is, How much can you do to ensure your survival when
it happens at your company—if it hasn't happened already?
Obviously, you can't go up to your supervisor and say, "Teach
me all you know, just in case." But keep your ears open, learn
how your department fits into the overall corporate picture.
Ask your supervisor to recommend related courses to take at a
local university. Ask to be included in departmental meetings
(arrange to trade phone duty with other friendly assistants so
they can attend their own departmental meetings). Then trade
the results of those meetings with the other assistants so you
all know what's happening.

3. *Managing diversity.* The Department of Labor esti-
mates that during the 1990s, nonwhites accounted for nearly
one third of all new office workers. This covers African-Ameri-
cans, Asians, and Hispanics. No matter who you are, what race

you belong to, or what your first language is, make an effort to include members of other populations in your informal social and business groups. Learn a second language. Then you'll be able to tell your own diversity story in two different languages!

4. *Understanding and using computers.* Ask for extra training in the latest technology, especially technology that specifically relates to the profession you work in. Imagine how that same technology is applicable to other professions and you've at least doubled your marketability!

5. *Teams.* The trend toward teamwork could be one of the most promising developments over the last few years of this century. Remember King Arthur's Round Table? He wanted it round so that no one would be at the head. He was still the king, but all the knights had an equal say in the way Old England would be laid out and managed. The same principle works, more or less, with teams. You'll still be the assistant, but assuming the other team members know how to make the best of the team concept, your voice will have the same impact and carry the same weight as that of those who appear higher up on the organization chart. It's a great way to get noticed.

6. *Service obsession.* This is an economy that's driven on information and customer service. Package your duties and present your accomplishments in those terms, and your supervisors and interviewers will see clearly that you are a results-oriented employee who considers the job done only when the customer—whether that person is internal or external—says thanks.

7. *Knowledge industries.* As we've transformed the U.S. countryside from smoking factories to low, sleek, gleaming office campuses, we've also shifted the emphasis on which skills are valuable. It's no longer how much you can lift, sew, or piece together. It's how much you know, and how quickly you can acquire new knowledge. Yeager and Hough write, "It is the belief of many in corporate America that intellectual capital rather than physical capital will be the driving force behind

the successful companies. People who can manage information well will be the stars. Demonstrating an understanding of organizational systems in all their forms; of telecommunications; and as mentioned earlier, of computers, both hardware and software, will set the smart applicant apart from the crowd.''

8. *Quality.* Know it well, but then be able to produce it so it's safe and sound. The U.S. automotive industry, looking over its shoulder at foreign car makers chipping away at their markets, really took the concept of quality to new levels when they actually used the term in their advertising campaigns. Whether you are producing a report or a nuclear reactor, poor quality wastes resources, reputations, and possibly puts people in danger. Any time you improve a product or a process by the slightest smidgeon, be sure to document it in your office records or task log (which you'll read about later). The reminder will come in handy while you're negotiating for a raise, a transfer, or a new job.

9. *Human resources.* All the automation in the world won't insulate us from dealing with humans now and then. No man is an island, remember? Yeager and Hough write, ''The successful organizations will be the ones that are able to hang on to valuable people. By showing your . . . employer that you have an understanding of human motivation and know how to keep other employees happy, you present yourself as someone who could be a potential solution to a looming problem of employee shortages.''

10. *Value-added.* If you are working in a corporate department that can show no direct contribution to the company's bottom line, it's time to get started figuring out how it saves the company money. For hints on where to begin, take a look at all these other trends. There is money buried in every one of them. Create an impact with these trends and you'll soon find the savings. Employees who can't put their finger on how they help the company actually do business will find themselves being asked to take themselves to another business.

11. *Ethics.* Every month a new business scandal hits the headlines. And we scratch our heads and ask, "What could they have been thinking?" You'd think that right and wrong are obvious. But they don't seem to be, since indictments are handed out these days like party favors. Know what your personal code of ethics is, and interview prospective employers accordingly. (The next time you start the job search, you might want to read Chapter 10, "Interview for a Values Match").

12. *Risky business.* Think of business as a knife. Resounding success and crushing failure are the two surfaces of the blade. And that sharp thing in the middle is your competitive edge. It takes nerve to keep your edge honed. Sometimes you draw the blade too much on one side, and not enough on the other. Whether your results are successes or failures, each swipe of the blade is a learning experience. Either way, give yourself credit for the nerve you mustered up to keep that knife sharp. And be ready to tell that story to supervisors and prospective employers. Whether it was a success or a failure, the way they interpret your story will tell you more about them.

These are the twelve trends in the nation's business climate today. Every time you make a decision or prioritize your day, see if there's a good correlation between your decision or priority and these trends. If not, maybe you can find a better choice—for both your company and your career.

—————— PROFILE ——————

Nancy Johnson
Administrative Assistant
Marriott Corporation
Bethesda, MD

When my husband was leaving the Navy twenty years ago, he was offered a job in Maryland. Since I'd chosen not to work while he was in the Navy, I needed to do something to bring my skills up-to-date. So I started out in a small electronics firm. But the company was so small, and so tightly disciplined, that I couldn't even get a new pencil without turning in the old one. I felt like I couldn't grow at all. And then I heard about Marriott from a friend at a party.

When I first interviewed, I was actually forgotten! My interview was at 1:00 P.M. I did my typing test, and then waited and waited and waited. I thought that maybe this was part of the test, to see how I responded under stress. Would I get mad and leave? Sure enough, I had been forgotten. The interviewer came rushing into the reception area, so apologetic. And then she said there was an opening in the compensation department, and that I could interview with the man immediately.

He was very nice. And nice is important to me. He offered me the job right there and then. Coming from that small company where I knew where everything was, I was totally overwhelmed by how large Marriott was. It took me a good year to feel comfortable. During that time I came to know about Cliff Ehrlich, the senior vice president of human resources. Even from the start, when I was filling out my benefits form, he came up and introduced himself. Here he was, a very important man, taking the time to introduce himself to me, a new secretary!

One day, I prepared the department's quarterly report in the wrong format. My boss was very upset. He said Mr. Ehrlich needed it right away and that I should immediately change the report and run it right over to him. As I was on my way to Mr.

Ehrlich's office, I spotted him walking across the parking lot. So I hollered, "Mr. Ehrlich! Mr. Ehrlich!" as I raced over to him. He just stopped in his tracks and calmly said, "Whatever it is, nothing is that important." Cliff didn't even turn around to see who it was he was talking to.

Eventually, I changed departments and went to work for a man who had the reputation of being very performance-oriented, demanding, and fast-paced. It wasn't always easy working with him, and it wasn't always pleasant. But I learned a lot, and, although I didn't realize it at the time, working at that level of the corporation prepared me for working with Cliff later.

I heard about the opening in Cliff's office because someone was nice enough to call me and tell me to apply. The job openings are always posted internally, but I would never have known the job was available. I was so swamped with work, I never would have even looked up to see what was going on around me.

Part of the process of applying for a new job internally is that you need to have a card signed by your current supervisor. When I handed it to my boss, he got really mad and threw it across the room. I could have justified my request by telling him how unhappy I was in that high-pressure environment and how I'd been spending day and night at work. But that wouldn't have impressed him.

So I just told him that the new job would mean a promotion from hourly to lower-level management. That did the trick. With him it wasn't sufficient to *feel* one way or the other. You had to back up your business decision by the results you expected from the change.

Working with Cliff was a totally different experience. He was always so calm about things. I had to learn that when he said, "Could you do this for me right away," that meant, "I want it right now."

He was always so kind and thoughtful. You didn't ever want to let him down. There's company loyalty, and then there's loyalty to your boss. I'm happy to say I've had both.

I've had a number of people come up to me and say, "You're so good, you should be in management." I'm happy to be an administrative assistant. And I owe a large part of the respect I got within the organization to the way he treated me. I was respected because he treated me with respect. Everyone took their cue from him.

But the years went by and he started talking more and more about his retirement. I thought I was ready for it, but I really wasn't. I was in denial. I kept thinking something would happen, that he might just semiretire, or work part-time in another executive office and take me with him. I didn't believe he was actually going until we had this big retirement party for him.

Managing the party was one of the hardest things that I'd ever done emotionally. But it was one of the easiest things I'd ever done in terms of planning. Afterward, everyone congratulated me on a beautiful party. But all I had to do was pick up the phone and say who the party was for. Everyone wanted to do their best.

I think that maybe I should have taken a few months off after Cliff retired, just to help myself with the transition. But I needed to clear out his office and get the department ready for his replacement. I didn't stay in that position because the new person was bringing his secretary up through the ranks with him.

It was also important for the next step in my career to be associated with Cliff as long as I could, even though he was officially retired. It still gave me the access I needed to the upper echelons of the company. But you can't bask in reflected glow for very long. I've got a new position now. But I still haven't really made up my mind what's next for me.

I have a ten-year-old son. And the other day he asked me, "How is your friend Mr. Ehrlich?" Not "How is that cranky, mean man you work with?" No, it was "How is your *friend?*" It makes me very happy to know that my experience is giving my son a good example of what a warm working relationship is all about.

Working with Cliff has made me a better employee, a better parent, and a better person.

My advice is:

1. *Get in an organization that's interesting to you.* It will be easier to get to know the company and make contacts that will see you throughout your career.

2. *When you meet a top-level person whom you admire, introduce yourself.* Say "I'd like to work for you one day." Make it clear that you aren't after anyone's job but that if the opportunity should present itself, you would like to be considered.

3. *Make good contacts with people who are currently executive assistants.* They are the first to know when good opportunities arise at the company's higher levels.

7

THRIVE? . . . OR MERELY SURVIVE? IT'S YOUR CHOICE

Sometime in early 1997, one of the television networks produced a newsmagazine program entitled, "Bad Bosses." The stories were about abusive individuals who wielded unfair power over their employees and made their lives a nightmare. "Why didn't you just quit?" asked one of the television reporters of a young woman who sat hunched, sad, and small over her kitchen table. "There was nowhere else to go," she murmured, without even looking up into the eyes of the reporter.

Don't you believe it! There is always a place to go!

This is not just a matter of faith. The national employment numbers almost everyday prove my point.

When it comes to what it means to be an employee today, there seem to be two channels of belief broadcasting throughout the country. On the one hand, you've got statistics that show companies are begging for qualified, self-motivating employees. Unemployment is lower than it has been in twenty-four years. Companies have stepped up their recruitment efforts to create even more of a hiring crunch. Do you want a job? All you have to do is take the help-wanted sign out of the employer's front window and walk right in.

There is also a skills gap in the job market today. Employers are stepping up their training programs to attract employees who have the potential but not necessarily the skills they need to hit the job running.

Then you have employers and peers—maybe even you—who think good jobs are hard to come by. That for every opening, there's a long line of candidates—many of whom are overqualified for the job. Remember the scene in *Mary Poppins* with all those nannies waiting to be interviewed for the position at the Banks' household? That's what I picture every time I think about this perspective on the chance of finding happiness with a really terrific job at a really terrific company. I mean, what are the chances? By the time you get to the head of the line, the job would be filled many times over. And that's not even counting the chance that Mary Poppins might swoop in and literally blow everyone else away.

Whatever channel you choose to believe, it will be true for you. So why not focus on the channel that says a world of opportunities is opening up to you? And, if you don't have the skills, all you have to do is show up, show interest, and tell the recruiter, "Show me the way and I'm there."

There's more good news. You have the ultimately portable career. You can take it anywhere! You want to live in Kaui but you're stuck in Kokomo, or vice versa? Well, they need office assistants in both places. You love your work, and at night you have season tickets to the Knicks? Sports teams need support staff. Have a knack for knockwurst? Learn a little German and check the employment listings in Munich.

As *Find Your Calling, Love Your Life* author Martha Finney says, "Work can be high adventure, or a calming refuge in a life full of personal challenges." No matter what you want out of your career, the workplace is a common ground for dreams to come true. As much as you are willing to keep your standards high and specific, you will be able to find an employer that wants to meet your expectations.

Or you may discover that your current employer is really "the one" and all this time you didn't know it because you hadn't figured out what was important to you and exactly how you wanted to live your life.

Whether you stay with your current employer, or find a new position elsewhere, it's all the same to me. My job here is to help you discover yourself, what your current skills are, what your potential is, what your dreams are, and what your limitations are.

And then you can set out on one of the biggest, most rewarding adventures of your life!

8

EXACTLY WHAT DO YOU THINK YOU'RE DOING?

I love the newspaper. You just never know what you're going to read about each day when you unfold that packet of paper, and start getting newsprint on your hands. The other day, while relaxing over the Sunday Style section of the *Washington Post*, I happened to lose myself in an article about an undertaker.

Not just any undertaker, you understand, but one who is also a poet. He lives in a town that's so small that whenever he walks into the local coffee shop and scans the room, he sees families and friends of people he has already taken care of. That's quite an intimate relationship with an entire town, don't you think?

At one point in the article he thinks aloud about what he does. "You might say I sell boxes," he says. And that he does, from a $79 cardboard item to a casket that sells for almost $8,000. All destined for the same place in the long run.

But that's not what he really does, he goes on to say. He says his job gives him the opportunity to give his townspeople comfort, patience, and a caring audience just when they need it most. The box business is really just a sideline in the final analysis.

So, what do *you* sell? Do you sell typing, just keystrokes on a computer? Do you sell the hours you spend occupying that chair you're sitting in? Do you sell your ability to alphabetize, spell, run spreadsheets, or answer the phone politely? Do you sell your punctuality?

Or are those really just sidelines?

All those skills and attributes are extremely important. And this isn't to put down your excellent talents and hard-won knowledge. But if you're not looking up and beyond your current set of skills to see how they fit into some bigger picture, you are cheating yourself of the pleasure of being at work.

Author Martha Finney says there are only three reasons why money changes hands. Imagine that, only three:

1. To relieve pain
2. To restore hope
3. To bring beauty and joy into the world

That's it. Only three reasons. All the rest is just embellishment. Every time you take out your wallet, whether to pay your electric bill, buy a bunch of carrots, or fill your gas tank, you're doing it for one or more of those three reasons. And behind each activity, there's at least one company, with its own cadre of office professionals.

So let's look at that undertaker again for just a moment. Which of those three needs does he respond to? Probably all three, wouldn't you say? Hmmm. It's easy to see how he relieves pain: He helps suffering families in their time of greatest emotional need. He restores hope by being there to talk about what happens to us when we die.

Bringing beauty and joy into the world, that's a toughie. Well, it's a beautiful moment when he holds a hand that needs to be held. Or when he offers comforting distraction to a child who might be just a little overwhelmed by all the sad goings-on. Have you ever seen one of those beautiful cemeteries? They're more like peaceful parks, offering just the serenity that we living need now and then. And offering habitats for song-birds, flowers, and butterflies—all there to remind us of the beauty of living. Our undertaker friend is part of the community of professionals who make those parks happen.

So what does this have to do with you? Well, maybe coincidence has it that you happen to be an undertaker's administrative assistant. But most likely not.

But what *does* your company sell that you support by investing your time and talents in its day-to-day operation? That's what you're selling also, simply by being associated with your employer. You might be tempted to say, "Oh I work at one of those huge conglomerates, there's nothing special about my job."

I don't think so. Say you work with a business that supports the farming industry. Well, we all know that most of the U.S. farms today are huge corporate enterprises. So big deal, right? Wrong. You are still an important part of the team that brings food to the table of families all around the world.

Or you work as a part-time administrative assistant at a tire store. Big deal, right? Wrong. You are part of an important team that helps people stay safe on the highways.

Or you are a receptionist at one of those software companies that seem to spring up and make a million dollars overnight. So are you really just part of a big money machine? Maybe. But these companies are increasingly important to the economy, especially regional economies. And the income those software engineers bring home—the income *you* bring home for that matter—goes a long way to support local businesses and your community's cultural, art, and learning enterprises.

John Donne wrote, "No man is an island, entire of itself; every man is a piece of the continent, a part of the main." The same can be said of businesses; we're all connected in a huge web of give and take. And a lot of administrative support has to go into that web.

Just think for a second about our undertaker friend again, going into a coffee shop for a quick breakfast with his neighbors. How many office professionals are behind that picture? They are there in the company that manufactured the suit he's wearing; in the construction company that built the restaurant; at the distributorship that delivers the farm-fresh eggs; at the restaurant supply company that provides the plates, flatware, and paper napkins. At the huge corporation next door that is the town's major employer.

They may think they're in business to make money, but all of these companies are part of a huge network to relieve pain, restore hope, and bring joy and beauty into the world. That's not a bad job description or corporate mission, if you ask me.

So, what is your company's corporate mission? If it doesn't have one that's formally published, can you figure it out and write it down in one or two sentences? Is that a mission you can stand behind and discuss proudly at the next party you go to?

I bet it is.

9

... And Why Do You Think You're Doing It?

Now that we've taken a quick look at how your company meets the needs of society, and how your career supports the company, let's focus on how your career *supports your life*.

Where's the mystery? you're probably wondering. Your career supports the roof over your family's head, food on the table, bus fare for you, and schoolbooks for the kids. Well, yes, all that's true. But if you stop there, you're robbing yourself of the chance to understand how the work you do today influences the way you feel about yourself and the way you set an example of hope and self-respect for everyone around you.

Let's face it, in the big picture scheme of things, the career of office professional doesn't get the most respect in the company. Just study the organizational chart, for example. Can you even find your position there? If your position is indeed listed, how many levels into the structure has it been buried? If you let your self-respect be determined by the way you are treated, or by the way you see your peers being treated, exactly how much respect would you have at the end of the day?

Not a whole lot, I suspect. Unless you happen to be one of the very lucky ones who landed a job with a savvy company that recognizes the ultimate value of keeping professionals like you on their payroll.

So your well of self-respect has to come from deep within you. No matter who your supervisor is, no matter what the office politics are, you must have your own unshakable core of self-worth and purpose in life.

Life's purpose: That's a pretty tall order, isn't it? Especially for an administrative assistant. Doctors have callings, you might be thinking. Lawyers, teachers, actors, all those highly paid and highly respected people—they're the ones with a calling.

And so are you. Remember Martha Finney's Big Three from the previous chapter? Relieve pain, restore hope, and bring joy and beauty into the world? Which one (or more) of those three things do you want to achieve in your life?

"Well, gosh," you might be thinking. "All I want to do is bring in an extra salary to help provide for my kid's college education fifteen years from now." That's what I call restoring hope. Wouldn't you agree?

Or maybe you're thinking, "I don't have any family, I live alone, this is a job to meet my basic needs, and I'm lucky if even that happens at the end of the month." Well, okay, it might seem like a skin-of-your-teeth existence to you now, but who do you suppose is watching you and drawing inspiration from the way you live your life every day? How much do you think that friendly guy at the fruit stand, or the bus driver, or the public librarian, or the check-out clerk would miss you if you didn't make your regular stop and say hello the way you've always done?

It may not seem like much right now, but it's a start. Maybe your current job is helping you bide your time as you grow into the magnificent creature you were meant to be. Gloria Estefan sings, "We're not just born to be alive." And we don't just work to *stay* alive. There is a greater meaning for the existence of each of us.

No matter what you do right now, consider what aspects of your work resonate with some mysterious urge deep within. Do you enjoy the feeling of being of service to others? Do you thrill at the prospect of meeting new people? Does the act of juggling crises electrify you? Are you a born problem-solver? Or (or *and*) do you like to collect people with a wide variety of talents and put their energies to work on some marvelous project?

Working in an office support function gives you the chance to discover and try all those career activities that delight you. Work, like every other aspect of your life, is a high adventure in self-discovery. And as you discover each new layer of capability and confidence, you are in a position of giving that much more to yourself, your family, your community, and even the world.

So you think helping the world is a really grandiose idea? And who are you to have such big ideas about yourself? Well, my question back at you is, Who are you *not* to have such big ideas?

You might as well. That's the first step to making those big ideas come true.

In his book *How to Find the Work You Love*, Laurence G. Boldt writes that "to fail to express your own talents is not only to deny your individuality, but to withhold from the world those special gifts which you possess."

And I intend to spend the rest of this book helping you to rethink your work as an office professional as an opportunity to exercise those wonderful talents you have within, and then reposition yourself as a valuable, confident player in your company, your community, and indeed in your own life.

Something to think about:

Gladys Holm was a retired secretary who never made more than $15,000 a year. When she died at age 86 in 1996 she left behind a small group of friends and a community of hospital volunteers who would forever remember her as the Teddy Bear Lady, because she always brought teddy bears to patients at the Children's Memorial Hospital in Evanston, Illinois. She also left an astounding donation to the hospital: $18 million that she earned during a lifetime of buying stock. That's $8 million more than even McDonald's founder Ray Kroc bequeathed the hospital.

Something to do:

Think about the reasons why you work. Is it to support your family? Pay for a college education for yourself or your children? To save enough money to buy an expensive luxury? Find a picture that symbolizes your current purpose and place it in a prominent position on your desk. So what if it's something materialistic like the red Cadillac Gladys Holms treated herself to, even as she was buying millions of dollars worth of stock. Being happy is a noble mission in life.

10

INTERVIEW FOR A VALUES MATCH

Susan, age 23, thought she had found her dream job when she landed a position in the membership department of an animal rights society. Fresh out of a southern college and new in New York City, she couldn't believe her luck in finding such a perfect job that suited her values. Cruelty prevention was one of them. Having a midtown office with a huge window overlooking the East River was really exciting.

The dream came crashing down one day near Christmas, when her supervisor came swooping into the office wearing a fur coat. "Look what [the society's president] gave me for Christmas," said Susan's boss. "Next year, I hope it will be a seal coat."

From that moment on, Susan no longer worked at the society. Sure, she showed up, but she left her heart at home in the morning. Within a couple of months, she gained a lot of weight, broke up with her boyfriend, and hightailed it back home to live with her parents for a couple of years while she sorted out this fresh set of realities in the workplace.

Now, I'm not about to discuss the relative merits of fashion fur—that's your business. But the point is that Susan found herself working in a organization that was completely inconsistent with its public image, and the absolute opposite of Susan's definition of right and wrong. Susan suffered what I call a capability crisis, which was brought on by a values clash. The fur coat incident changed her relationship with her employer, absolutely. But what really brought her down was having to come to terms with the cold truth that all is not consistent—or honest or fair—in business. So, the challenge became for her—as it does for all of us at one time or another—to discover exactly what was important to her personally and how much she would have to compromise that value in exchange for a regular paycheck.

The good news is that there is probably no better time in the history of work when you *can* match your values with your paycheck. As we've already seen, the demand for qualified employees is high, so you can pick and choose. And values-based decision making in business is increasingly respected. Look, investors can do it. There are plenty of mutual funds that share a common ethic beyond simply making money: They will buy shares only in companies that mirror their principles both through their public policies and their actions, whether it's civil rights, environmental concerns, or developing impoverished nations.

So if investors can do it, you certainly should be able to do it in your job search. After all, every day you spend on the job in effect makes you an investor. You may not be buying any shares with cash in the conventional way. But you're buying a stake in the company with your time. You definitely have a vested interest in what the company does and how it treats people.

Okay, so maybe you're not necessarily up on the burning issues of the day. Or you're wondering how your particular job at your particular company affects people in, say, Algeria, or the pink dolphins in the Amazon (yes, there are such things). Well, maybe it doesn't. But the environment at work either poisons or benefits the ecology of *your* life. So when you look in the mirror after a long day at work, do you see a happy face bursting with health and confidence? Or do you see a polluted field of sadness and conflict?

If you don't like what you see, it's time for a change. Psychologists say that a poor employment match, one that is against your most genuine nature, leads to illness, stress, unhealthy sleep and eating habits, and even drug and alcohol abuse. Not to mention an employment record of tardiness and sick leave, which could get you fired and leave you with bad job references to bring into your future. So, maybe it's time to start looking for a new position if you see that level of unhappiness in the mirror.

You're probably wondering how you could possibly grill prospective employers on their values. Put yourself in Susan's position. Can you imagine her asking her potential supervisor if she would ever wear a fur coat if the boss were to give her one? Considering the fact that she had been interviewing for an animal rights job, it's a fair bet to say the subject probably wouldn't have even come up.

Sure, you can't uncover all the possible mismatches during an interview. And really, in hindsight, it would be best for Susan to chalk up the experience to just plain bad luck and learn not to let it get her down. But there are plenty of things you can do before, during, and after a job interview that will help improve your chances of finding a position in a company that most closely matches your sense of what's right and wrong.

First of all, know your own set of values and needs. What is an absolute must for you? Is it important for you to identify so closely with the company's mission that you would tattoo it on your shoulder? Or maybe it just would be nice to work at a company that is *clear* on what its mission is. Is courtesy a two-way street for you? How about the ideal office environment? Do you prefer it to be a casual, congenial place that promotes team creativity? Or do you like to be left alone to come up with your own solutions to work problems?

You'd think that by the time we're old enough to go on job interviews, we'd also be mature enough to know these things about ourselves. No matter how old we are, it's important to revisit these kinds of questions every few years. As we become more seasoned—through our work and our private lives—our work styles and preferences change, without our even realizing it.

For the purposes of this book, I'm assuming that you are at least expecting a workplace environment that practices a respect for the personal dignity of all its employees (not just senior management) and that will encourage you to develop yourself to your full potential. Even if it's at the risk of your ultimately leaving the firm for better opportunities elsewhere.

When you're interviewing a potential employer, you are evaluating the company as much as you're marketing yourself. It's a matching expedition for both of you. The power to accept or reject is equally shared. Bear that in mind as you walk into your appointments and you've taken an important step in positioning yourself as an "employee of choice" looking for an "employer of choice."

What you want to see during the interview process is evidence of a work environment that promotes and supports both self-respect and mutual respect.

Before the interview, make sure you know what the company stands for. We discuss researching a company elsewhere in this book, but at this stage it's especially important to make sure the company's actions match its stated values. Read the front matter of its latest annual report. Each year a company highlights a new theme that best reflects the position the company wants to associated with. "People are our best asset" is a popular one, but it is so overdone and so hackneyed that you might want to look twice at its turnover and downsizing record over the last couple of years. Community volunteerism is another popular theme.

The front part of the annual report is designed to make potential investors feel good about supporting the company. So take it with a grain of salt, and match its message to its actual record over the past two years or so. If you're not comfortable doing Internet research, and if juggling reels of microfilm turns you off the prospect of searching back issues of newspapers in the library, take heart. That's what the news magazines are for, as far as I'm concerned. Look up the company's name in the *Reader's Guide to Periodical Literature*, and you'll likely find references to the company in *Newsweek*, *Time*, *Fortune*, *Forbes*, or any number of the popular and easy-to-read magazines.

If mission and record match, you're in luck. If they don't, well at least you'll have something interesting to talk about during your interview. So what about that executive who appeared on the news program *60 Minutes* and said that cigarettes were no more addictive than Gummy Bears candy? What about that unfortunate incident involving bras, lampshades, and spike heels at the annual board meeting? How did the firm handle that nasty old class action suit last year? Did that nationwide recall result in any drop in stock prices? Did *that* result in any downsizing? Ask a sticky question. Do it nicely. Do it politely. And if the interviewer still gets defensive or edgy, you've tapped a nerve and uncovered a problem.

Or maybe you found an example of the company's mission in action. How about that six-figure contribution to an organization of volunteer plastic surgeons who donate their vacation time to help Third World children? Or wasn't that a great marketing idea to offer $1,000 to Rosie O'Donnell's favorite children's charity every time she gets kissed during her television show? Find out what makes a company proud. Talk about why it makes the company proud. And maybe even brainstorm with your interviewer ways the company can repeat that success.

Isn't that what interviews are for—to find a values match?

And all this time you thought interviews were for landing you a job.

Regardless of your personal values and ethics, there are some universal hallmarks of potential employers who stand a better chance of offering you happiness and dignity, as well as a paycheck you can count on and a career you can build. Don't be afraid to keep your own mental checklist; the guy who's interviewing you has one he's filling out about you.

1. *Is the employer on time for his or her interview appointment with you?* Lisa, in Seattle, waited for an hour and a half for a morning interview, only to be told that the interviewer had just been called into a meeting with the CEO and wouldn't be available to meet with her until late in the afternoon. And would she please come back? "Sure," she said. And returned later, killing time by going to an early matinee. By the time she returned, the interview had been postponed until

the following week. She got the interview all right. But didn't hear from the company until three months later when she got a letter saying the position had already been filled. Oh, how I wish she had told the company that first morning that she was no longer interested in employment with that firm. It would have done her pride wonders.

No matter how much you want the job or want to work for that company, don't wait more than twenty minutes for a scheduled interview without receiving an explanation or apology. If they don't respect you when you're a visitor, they won't respect you when you're an employee.

2. Is your interviewer attentive and imaginative, and does he or she speak to you as an adult? Employers who keep up with the latest trends and techniques realize that it takes more to find a good match than simply running down a line of pre-established questions on a printed sheet of paper. The quality employer is just as interested in getting a values match as you are. Instead of an interrogation, the interview should be more of a relaxed conversation in which you have the chance to tell stories about your past experiences, the challenges you faced, and how you successfully handled them.

An imaginative, creative interview will reflect an excellent chance that your tenure in that company will also be imaginative and creative, giving you all sorts of opportunities to grow from exciting experiences.

3. If you are involved in a team interview (where members of your prospective department get to know you or you are speaking with a cross-functional group), does everyone agree with the company's mission and prospects? Cary, age 36, went to a team interview in Silicon Valley for a support position for a team that was engineering a new CD-ROM product. (Team interviews are popular in high-tech companies because creative chemistry and cohesiveness must be counted on during crunch times, say at 1 A.M. when the engineers have just finished their fifth pizza and have finally buckled down to work.) Half the team members interviewing Cary told her straight out that they saw no future in the product and that it was a loser from the beginning. She chose not to accept that company's job offer.

The flip side of that experience is what happens at Industrial Light and Magic, where employees will actually take a *pay cut* to work with George Lucas on his spectacular film projects, such as the *Star Wars* series. Candidates who want to work at his studios must also participate in group interviews. But there they hear about how dynamic the creative atmosphere is and about the exciting A-list clients that Lucas attracts. Any candidate who is a good values match at Industrial Light and Magic is welcomed into the group, and there are very few missteps and mishirings.

While we're on the subject of team interviews, if you are participating in a cross-functional interview, in which the team members represent all departments of the company, is there at least one member of the support staff on the interviewing team? The presence of office professionals on a selection team says a lot about the company's attitude toward its support staff. It shows that the company values the opinions of support members, even when hiring technical or managerial employees. And since participating in a selection team is a great career move and a chance to help build the company, it shows that the employers respect the personal ambitions of their support professionals.

That's an excellent sign of your prospects for happiness there.

4. *Is there is any difference in the training and educational opportunities for support staff as opposed to the managerial or technical staff?* There probably is. Let's face it, right or wrong, companies consider their investment to be in the higher level employees. But what you want to learn is exactly how wide that gap is. Then it's up to you to decide if that gap is tolerable.

Try to get examples of support-level employees who were able to train themselves into higher, better-paying positions. Now, you're probably thinking, "I can't appear too ambitious or the company will think I'll want out of the job as fast as I get into it."

Yes, there are companies like that and there are interviewers with that mentality. Those are *not* the companies you want to work with. Yes, they have needs to fill and functions they're counting on you to perform. And, yes, they probably don't relish the prospect of having to fill your job over and over again. And those are legitimate concerns.

What you want is an employer who knows that the best way to retain valued employees is to train them. And that allowing *you* to manage your career according to your own personal goals and values is the best way to keep excellent, motivated, self-starting talent. The best way to keep you. And there are plenty of employers out there just wondering when someone like you will finally walk through their doors and sit down for the chat that will change both your destinies.

After the interview, enjoy the day. Do something that makes you feel as though you can afford all the time in the world to make this important decision. For instance, go on another interview. Have lunch with a friend who works at an exciting company. Go for a run. Go back to work and volunteer for a dynamic project. Keep all your appointments, and expect people to keep theirs with you. Take your mind off the interview by moving yourself forward in another aspect of your life.

By the next day, of course, make sure your thank-you note is in the mail. But then go on with your life, taking all the time *you* need to decide for yourself whether you will take the job when it's offered. Eventually the phone will ring, and a values-based match will be offered that will change your life.

And change the face you see in the mirror after a long day of work. A face that reflects genuine self-respect is one of your best career assets.

---------------- **PROFILE** ----------------

Ginnie Helin
Corporate Giving Manager
Lands' End
Dodgeville, WI

I was hired in January 1979 to help type refund checks as a part-time job. At that time Lands' End was a really small company, and I didn't give a second thought to its prospects for growth. I was really just looking for part-time work, and I wanted something besides babysitting. But because of my secretarial background, I never did work a part-time shift. And I was eventually exposed to every function of the organization.

Whenever a new function needed to get started, I was the one they tapped for the job. I helped set the company up when it moved from the original building into the new facilities. I ended up doing the interviewing and the hiring for every department. When the company installed the new computerized phone system, I was the one they sent to Texas for the two-week course on how to maintain the system. When word processing was started, I developed that department and became its supervisor. I got housekeeping and maintenance started. And when we moved into the second building, I developed the facility planning department. That's where I stayed when they hired the vice president for facility planning.

Then the corporate giving function came to me. This was a very, very big job, but it wasn't formally organized yet. So in 1992, I said, "Let's develop a corporate giving department." So I was asked to develop a written policy, set up a corporate giving committee, and report directly to the senior vice president.

The funny thing is, although I'm manager of the corporate giving department, I am also the administrative assistant to the vice president of operations. And I have a secretary myself!

Of all the jobs I've had, this is one I like the best. I tell my boss that when he retires I'm retiring too. He's very sensitive to you and flexible when it comes to family needs. That attitude is the same throughout Lands' End. They know that your family is the most important thing to you. And if there's something your kids need you for, you go.

I never followed a career path here. I just did my best. And everything that happened to me fell into place. But if you are interested in another job within Lands' End, they keep a Job Enrollment binder that lists all the jobs within the company— along with the skills, knowledge, and experience required for the job. If you want to someday do that job, you tell your supervisor that that's what you're aiming for. And together you start making plans in that direction. The University of Wisconsin even has courses here.

My advice is:

1. *As you climb, encourage the people who will be coming after you.*

2. *Be open to taking on new assignments, even when they come out of the blue.* When you say no, no one will ever come back to you with new assignments. That doesn't mean you have to take an assignment that's wrong for you. But you should be able to explain to your supervisor exactly why you don't want an assignment.

3. *If you find yourself working for a new boss who has been hired from outside, help your boss succeed by teaching him the culture.* Lands' End is a special place that's built on trust and respect for all employees. Sometimes newcomers come in with a more conventional way of doing things. Frequently, their success depends on a considerate secretary who lets them in on the Lands' End culture.

11

HAVE YOU OUTGROWN
YOUR OWN IMAGE?

Not yourself today?

Have you ever looked in the mirror and felt like screaming, "Help! I'm trapped in the body of the person I used to
be!" Oh, yes, I know you have. Our external world is always
several paces behind our internal changes and improvements.
That's natural and logical, simply because real advancement
has to happen inside first in order to stick. Unfortunately, we
tend to get so bogged down with the work of growing that we
forget to re-evaluate from time to time the world immediately
surrounding us to make sure it still matches. Consequently
our external message frequently tends to be at odds with the
direction we want to achieve.

Look in your closet, for instance, and check out the
clothes. Maybe there are a few new pieces that more accurately
express who you are today, but—unless you're Ivana Trump—
I'm guessing the bulk of your wardrobe is that same old serviceable stuff that still looks decent, unspotted, tear-free.

So you continue to wear it. On a limited salary, that's the
only frugal, smart thing to do, right? Wrong.

You'll find that this kind of penny-wise behavior is costing
you huge dividends in confidence and positioning in the career marketplace. You've changed over the years. You've
grown, matured, and expanded your ideas of what you can
make for yourself in life. But if you're still wearing the clothes
you selected before you focused on new levels of ambition,

your old outside image is holding back the new, blossoming you.

I'm not telling you to go out and break the bank at your favorite clothes store. Right now, I'm only using clothes as a *symbol* of the *many* aspects of life that you've outgrown. Other things might also be telling lies about who you've grown to become. The little doodads and artwork around your desk. Your company, maybe. Your job description. Your idea of what your limitations are. And yes, I'm afraid, maybe even some of your friends—not all of them, but certainly some of your friends.

It's natural to grow out of the things we used to love. We are meant to *build* on our past, not accumulate it. And in this chapter I'm going to show you how to clean out a few of the many closets in your life, both literally and figuratively, leaving room for new and wonderful expressions of what you've grown to become—and how you're still growing.

ALL THE THINGS YOU ARE

YOUR CLOTHES

When it comes to clearing out the wardrobe, there are two popular pieces of advice. But I think they only begin the process of truly updating the message your clothes say about you. So I'll take you through them, and then beyond.

The first piece of advice is, "Get rid of anything you haven't worn in one/two/four/five years." Okay, I'd agree with that, but only if you really detest the item or if it no longer fits you. But, before you pitch it, take a fresh approach to those old clothes, the older the better. What old dreams and passions do they represent for you? As you've moved up in the career world, for instance, did you stop wearing that packable dress from Banana Republic? Did that dress once appeal to your sense of high adventure? In your mind's eye did you imagine how cool and airy it would be when someday you walked through the streets of Cairo with a capuchin monkey

riding on your shoulder? Or those old lime green pedal push-
ers from Esprit de Corps. They always reminded you of a lively
California lifestyle. But as you more frequently forgot to wear
them in favor of easy chinos, did you also forget your dream
to someday move to San Francisco?

Fashion marketers have always appealed to our fantasy
lives. Just look at the advertisements in magazines. We know
rationally that few people really live like that. But how many
of us would want to at least taste that kind of life? So we buy
their clothes. It follows that much of the fashion you have selected over the years somehow appealed to some of your best
daydreams. Look through your closet and try to recapture
some of those big ideas that you put away in favor of a so-
called secure job. Now that we know secure jobs aren't that
secure anymore, we might as well dust off the big ideas again.

Maybe you finally have everything you need to make
those original dreams come true: skills, experience, and contacts. And maybe it's just possible that a San Francisco-based
import/export firm specializing in Egyptian jewelry is looking
for an executive assistant right now, with a "willingness to
travel preferred." If such a life still appeals to you, this is a
dream that you won't grow out of. So make yourself happy
and give in to it. And get that dress back in the closet.

Don't throw away your dreams, even if they are a little
snug. They can always be let out.

The second piece of advice is to "dress like your boss (or
some other variation of the theme of dressing for the job you
want to have). Whose big idea was that? I don't know anyone
who can afford to dress like their boss. Since when can you
cough up the cash to buy cashmere-lined gloves, Coach brief-
cases, or Burberry raincoats? The status symbols of conventional corporate success are status symbols for a reason:
They're astronomically expensive! And if you buy knock-offs,
you run the risk of looking fake. The key for you is to invest in
the best possible quality of the kinds of clothes that make *you*
feel good—not clothes that so transparently play into someone else's ego.

And then find the career environment that responds to

your sense of outer self-expression. Here's a new twist on this rule, based on an old piece of advice from Henry David Thoreau: "Beware of all enterprises that require new clothes." Of the many ways to interpret that line, I prefer looking at it this way: If the job is a natural fit for you, your talents and interests, you probably already wear (or at least have) the appropriate kinds of clothes.

My personal twist is to carefully observe the kinds of clothes your potential boss is wearing when you are still in the job interview process. Is your prospective supervisor wearing pinstripes and tightly laced oxfords but you are your happiest and most productive in jeans, a cotton T-shirt, and running shoes? That should tell you something right there about the chances of your being happy and compatible with such a formal office set-up and get-up. Do you have your doubts that you can find an office environment that would be so casual? Head straight for the high-tech start-up companies. And don't make the mistake of assuming that such a high-risk employer offers no security. This country is full of support professionals who are now millionaires because they got in on the ground floor.

Likewise, if you have a more formal demeanor, look for an office environment that reflects that kind of attention to detail. If you are a pinstripes kind of person, you're going to quickly resent the wacky, chaotic atmosphere of most young high-tech start-ups.

This is a win/win situation that will take your career prospects to amazing levels of interest and material rewards. You will blossom best in an environment that's suited to your needs and temperament. And companies blossom best when their positions are filled by appropriate employees. Finger through your hangers, dig around in those drawers. Much of what you already wear (or have forgotten to wear) carries the secret of what will make you happiest at work.

Two more final points before we leave your closet. Let's say you've been sailing around the world for the last three years, so all you have are salt-stained jeans, flip-flops, and three T-shirts. Then one day, killing some time at some marina bar in Thailand, you pick up a copy of the *Wall Street Journal* and say to yourself, "Investment banking! That's for me!" I can tell you right now, jeans and T-shirts aren't going to cut it on Wall Street. But you already knew that, didn't you? I knew you did.

Talk about the high risk of investing in futures. It's not easy or inexpensive gearing up for a life of accelerated ambition.

So how do you get presentable? With these two words: consignment shops. You can pick up exquisite business suits and accessories for a fraction of their original price at these stores, which are springing up all over the country. This is where the wealthy recycle their cast-offs and can indulge in their own love of shopping. So strike up a conversation with the browsers at the rack next to you. You never know whom you're going to meet, who just so happens to know someone who just so happens to need someone just like you.

What about your jeans and T-shirts? If they've really been around the world with you, I'd say either frame them or burn them. But most of us regular folk have five or six office pieces that are in terrific condition; they just don't match our lives anymore. If they are in good shape, and *only* if they are in good shape, take them to any one of many charity options you have in your community, such as Goodwill, the Salvation Army, or a local dry cleaner that might be running a clothing drive.

This is especially important for the business suit you know you'll never wear again. That may be just the thing someone else needs to cinch his or her own job interview and move up out of unemployment and welfare.

Just think, you probably have three or four futures hanging right there in your closet. Good, serviceable futures someone else can use. And all this time you thought they were just your past.

Say the word "accessory" and we usually think scarves and jewelry. Say "desk accessory" and we think calendars and pencil cup holders. But how you equip your workspace says more about you than that.

Your Office

I read a magazine article once that said the more plastic you have on your desk, the lower your salary tends to be. That seems a little harsh—and my apologies to the plastics industry for perpetuating that little bit of snobbery.

Have what you like on your desk. But make sure you truly like what you have. As you grow, mature, and learn, your tastes change. And by now you might have outgrown those nifty knickknacks that were so perfect a year or two ago. But since they are familiar, you've probably stopped seeing them. So you've overlooked the fact they don't represent you anymore.

Cast an eye over your workstation. Does it tell the world who you are today, or who you were when you first took your position? Are its accessories compatible with your supervisor's office? Of course they don't have to match your supervisor's accessories pencil cup for pencil cup. And as with your supervisor's clothing, I'm not suggesting that you furnish your workspace with the same luxurious status appointments that your boss might have: leather chairs, silver trophies, or crystal statues. But if your boss is someone whose career path inspires you, you can modify your boss's taste to your budget. You don't have to be your boss's clone, but it's important to remember that most visitors will pass by your workstation, if not actually stop there, before entering your boss's office. So you definitely want your area to reflect the spirit of your team.

That cartoon of the laughing person saying, "You want it *when?*" won't serve your long-term interests of advancing your career to more interesting projects and higher salaries. Likewise, most books will tell you to keep a mirror or a sign that reads "Smile" by your phone. Excuse me, but if you're that demoralized or bored by the job that you can't even smile without being reminded, then I suggest you get either a new attitude or a new job. Either way, get rid of the reminder.

I advise my clients to place a picture illustrating "What's in it for me" prominently on their desks—the reasons why they come to work—such as a diploma, a retirement home, a boat, braces, or a ski vacation. Heck, how about food or an apartment? Many employers believe that the company's mission itself should be enough incentive for their workers. (File that under *Y* for "Yeah, right.") Mission statements are all very nice, but they won't put food on the table.

Avoid all slogans except for corporate messages or wisdom from the CEO. Your coffee mug should have an appropriate, pleasing design, with no unrelated messages that you might also find on T-shirts. Some companies tolerate, even encourage, those motivational posters. The photography is beautiful, granted, and the messages are inspiring. However, save them for your home office if you don't see them anywhere else in your organization. Someone might conclude that if you need to be motivated by posters for teamwork, striving, or success, you might be more easily motivated somewhere else.

The stores that sell those posters, however, also offer other, more subtle office accessories. Paperweights and books bearing quotes from great thinkers, for example, will give you moments of wisdom without broadcasting to the world that you need to look at pictures of runners and rowers to give yourself that extra boost of energy to get through the day.

Personalize your workstation with artwork, but choose examples of fine art, the kind you would find in galleries. Museums produce postcards of their most prominent pieces. Choose a wide variety that particularly appeals to you (or even relates to your industry somehow) and start your own collection. Timeless art never goes out of fashion.

Your calendar should also reflect your personal project of self-improvement. One of those word-a-day calendars will increase the range of your vocabulary. The same museum shops that sell postcards also have lovely calendars. A desk calendar that opens flat on a surface is preferable to a wall calendar. That way you keep your appointments and personal business to yourself.

Calendars can be pricey, particularly the top-quality ones. If your budget won't allow you to own an elegant calendar, here's a way you can get one for free: Contact your counterpart in any department, such as marketing, public relations, advertising, or editorial, that works with high-end print shops. These departments get swamped with free calendars from printers every year. And they're gorgeous, artistic, and inspiring. Printers rely on these calendars as their best year-round advertising. So they invest a lot of thought, creativity, and design talent in them.

PEOPLE

Finally, I want to touch on a more sensitive subject: the friends who surround you.

"Oh, no!" I can hear you saying. "Next she's going to tell me to ditch my friends! First my favorite mug and now my friends!"

Of course I wouldn't tell you to throw over your friends. And I certainly don't want to make light of a subject that can be very painful. But I will tell you to get rid of the so-called friends who in fact are saying behind your back, "Just who does she think she is?" And I think you have a pretty good idea who those people are.

Misery loves company. And misery will turn on you if you try to leave its parlor. Do you remember when Oprah Winfrey first lost all that weight? A lot of people were banking on her gaining it back. And others were actually *mad* at her for leaving their ranks of unhappiness and trying to make life better for herself.

It's one of those nasty little secrets about success that no one tells you about. Moving up into new circles means you will lose some friends, well, so-called friends. Some of these people are just mean-spirited and will hope that you fail utterly and return to their level, thereby justifying their own failure to try for something better themselves. I have experienced this personally, with my own friends and family.

Others just won't recognize you anymore. This is especially true among family members who liked you just the way you were. It worked for them; you fit into the family scheme of things. All of a sudden you don't. You've become way too big for your britches.

And there are still others who simply don't find you fascinating anymore. You don't speak the way they speak, your ideas are strange, and your hobbies have changed. They'll just fall away, and you'll hardly notice that you don't see them anymore until you're sitting down with your holiday card list and think to yourself, "Gee, how long has it been?"

But it's the first group that worries me, whose members won't let you be happy in your growth. Suddenly you'll discover that they are bringing you down, ever so subtly. They're not your friends. Repeat: *They're not your friends.* Simply say to them, "Thank you very much, but I don't see it that way anymore." And be on your way.

As for your family members, of course, you're stuck with them. You love them, and they love you. But even their words and actions can be particularly devastating if it becomes obvious that they're more interested in keeping you from growing for a particular reason. Love them. Appreciate them. Forgive them. But your future is yours alone, and your life is what you make of it.

George Bernard Shaw wrote: "The people who get on in this world are those who look for the circumstances they want. If they can't find them they make them."

Keep going down your road, and maybe someday soon they'll catch up.

You're not who you used to be. Enjoy your growth. Express your changes. And you'll find that your true friends and loving family will be with you, celebrating each step of the way. And taking your story as inspiration for their own growth.

12

EDUCATION IS STILL THE KEY TO THE FUTURE

By now I'm sure you're very clear that I'm big on self-determination. You are what you make of yourself. Way back in Chapter 4, I talked about you as Me, Inc. So we already know that you are your own corporation, right? Right.

You are also your own education. And now I want to talk about Me University.

As much as I am a cheerleader for self-determination, I also believe very strongly in the power of education. But perhaps not the kind of education you're used to thinking about. That formal, stuffy classroom with a stern and frowning instructor. That constant worry that you may not do well on the next exam or term paper. The ongoing pressure to make tuition payments.

I'm talking about the kind of education that lifts the ceiling of opportunity off your head and teaches you how to think differently about the life you're already leading. This kind of education opens doors: doors to higher salaries, doors to more promising employers, or maybe even doors to new and exciting places to live, and new and exciting people to be with. That's Me U. And you *can* get your college degree there.

If you have only your high school diploma—or even if you haven't made it that far—this chapter is for you. By the time you're done with the next few pages you will see that a college degree is definitely within your reach and that the rewards of better job opportunities and a higher salary will make the necessary effort very worthwhile.

There are so many reasons many of us interrupt our educations before achieving undergraduate degrees from accredited colleges or universities. But it basically boils down to an issue of priorities and limited resources.

- Maybe you were just bored with school. You couldn't see how any of your classes were "relevant" to the real world, so you dropped out. You got a taste of the real world, all right. And you discovered that the real world paid educated employees more than it was going to pay you.
- Maybe your family only had the tuition for one child to go on to college. And they didn't pick you.
- Maybe you got pregnant or your girlfriend got pregnant.
- Or maybe you knew yourself well enough to know you weren't ready for college and decided to temporarily postpone your freshman year. But somehow time flew and life's events overtook any ambition you might have had to return to the books full-time.

All these things can happen to smart, talented teenagers who truly deserve to get the education they need to live up to their potential. You keep thinking "someday," but in the meantime, you have no energy left at the end of the day to devote to hard study. Or the kids need braces, which takes that tuition money you've been setting aside. Or you just got divorced and need every extra penny to find a new place to live. One right after the other, life's events keep steering you away from that diploma.

And daily you witness the rewards of an education. You may have fifteen years' solid experience in an organization, but some young pup with a degree comes in at triple your salary. You might get passed over for a promotion that goes to someone who offers both experience *and* a degree. You might not get called in for an interview because the published job opening specifies a college graduate. In many cases a position that you would be perfectly suited for doesn't truly need a college background. But the people who write those job descriptions might not know that. And the phrase "college degree preferred" is so easy to type, why not throw it into the announcement, just for good measure?

It used to be that a college education was the sole privilege of the especially gifted or well-to-do. That's who we usually picture in our mind's eye when we think about campus life. But in truth, the college degree is so commonplace today that hiring managers expect you to have at least a bachelor of arts or a bachelor of science degree to keep your résumé in the stack of contenders for that job opening. On the one hand, we think of the college degree as a privilege of the elite. But on the other hand, employers expect us all to have one.

So there you are, selected out of opportunities, despite your gifts, talents, and experience, simply because you cannot step up to the plate called "college degree preferred." No it's not fair. But that's a fact of modern life.

Here's another fact of modern life: That college degree is within your reach! No matter who you are, no matter how old you are, or how much money you make or don't make, it's possible to work toward that degree and position yourself as a competitive candidate for those great new job opportunities that come along.

If it's a financial concern you have, there are many solutions to that problem. Perhaps your company has a tuition plan. Many companies will reimburse your education expenses provided you make at least a C and are in a course of study that's related to your work. Or investigate the residency requirements for your state university. Some state colleges are so well-funded that residents can get their college degree for a fraction of what a private college would cost.

There are also some marvelous scholarship programs that can help you meet expenses. And you don't even have to be a scholar to get a scholarship. Many programs were set up to support specific kinds of populations. In fact, I even heard of one once that offered a partial scholarship for young women who could prove they had Swedish ancestry. Scholarships take some time to research, but all you need is a friendly public librarian or admissions counselor. The two of you can take on the adventure of puzzling out your financial white knight together.

Time and convenience are two other factors that keep adults from returning to school. But colleges even have that one figured out in the form of *external degree programs.* This is your ticket to a better future.

Remember what a daunting prospect it was to compete for a limited number of acceptances in the "college of your choice"? In those days, all you could think about was the ratio of thousands of applications for only a few hundred openings in the school. Could you dare dream that your application package would be so outstanding that it would rise above everyone else's?

Things are different now in the college application marketplace. These schools are actually going after adult students, hoping to entice them back to school for continuing education programs (which are usually non-degree) and degree programs that will help them finally graduate. Why this change of heart among educational institutions? As an adult student you are more than just a source of added revenue to these schools. You also bring to the campus the seasoned perspective of someone who has been out in the real work world actually *doing* what the younger students are learning about.

That is, you would be if you went to the campus at all. Some external degree programs can be done from your dining room table if you want. In fact, some colleges, such as the Regents College in Albany, don't even have campuses at all. With these types of programs, you could be floating on an aircraft carrier in the middle of the Mediterranean for all they care.

These colleges are set up exclusively for adult students who want to achieve a degree to position themselves as competitive candidates for better jobs. Or maybe just for the satisfaction of finally earning that sheepskin. Whatever your motivation to finally be able to call yourself a college graduate, these colleges are there to help you get that degree.

The first step is an assessment and evaluation process to

measure what you have already achieved, and which can be accepted as college credit toward your degree. There are many ways you probably have already earned some valuable credits: traditional course credits, courses you have taken through your employer, military training, or correspondence courses, among others. In addition, the school can also help you convert real-life experience into college credit by giving you a chance to demonstrate that the knowledge you have in a specific area is equivalent to a college course. Just as there are high school equivalency tests, there are also college-level equivalency tests. Your school will help you identify opportunities to take those tests and convert your experience into college credit.

Then, once you've been assessed, the school will determine which courses you need to pass to qualify for its degree program. You can takes these courses either through your local college or through a correspondence course.

The beauty of these types of programs is that you can start when you want to and finish when you want to. My contact at Regents College tells me that among the 76,000 students that have graduated from Regents, one was a fourteen-year-old candidate for a bachelor of arts degree, and another was a seventy-nine-year-old woman who wanted the satisfaction of having completed her formal education.

But most are like you. The extra education and credibility that the diploma gives you will make you more competitive in the marketplace, with better prospects for financial reward, more security, and greater control over your own future.

And then *you* can determine how your career will be built.

The more education you have, the better position you're in to custom design your life and do *what* you want.

—————— PROFILE ——————

Barbara King
Account Executive
MasterCard International
Dover, DE

Nothing important in life happens exactly the way you plan it when you're eighteen. I started college but became totally disenchanted with the major I had chosen. I started out as a science major. But research money was being slashed in those days, and job prospects didn't look very good.

So I temporarily left school and went into banking instead, starting out as a teller. Eventually I was promoted to branch manager and loan officer. I stayed in banking for eight years and had a wonderful time. During that time I got married, and my new husband was transferred to Delaware.

This gave me the chance to finish my degree, and so I took a part-time clerical job at the University of Delaware. A university is a fun place to work. The collegiate atmosphere is very supportive, and anyone who proves herself can move up. Which is what I did, and I soon became the program manager for the American Bankers Association's National School of Bankcard Management. That gave me many connections within MasterCard and Visa and the credit card banking establishment.

These connections were the real linchpin for me. But my university days were coming to an end. Someone at Master-Card heard I was leaving the university and asked for my résumé on the spot.

Now I'm working as regional manager, which is half administrative support and half professional. I have a track record for turning positions into something else. If I started out right, I knew chances were good I could move up. I work with a wonderful, supportive group of people. They ask for my opinion; they discuss plans with me rather than lay out an order.

Make no mistake, I understand the chain of command. If someone needs to bark out an order, I understand and don't take offense.

A lot has to do with how I see myself. It doesn't make that much difference to me what my title is. I know what I'm doing, and that's more important to me than what's on my business card.

The words "that's not in my job description" have never passed my lips. Sure, I have been taken advantage of at times. But you know what? I've always come out on top. The five minutes I'm being taken advantage of now usually end up with a promotion later.

I've always enjoyed being part of a team. I try as often as possible to put myself in the other person's position. Sometimes it involves mind reading. I have a close working relationship with the senior vice president, who's an extraordinarily busy guy. When I see something that needs to be done, I just do it. Sometimes it's as mundane as emptying the trash. But sometimes I have to be the bearer of difficult news.

This is my advice:

1. *Believe in yourself and your capabilities.* If you don't, no else will.

2. *Take every opportunity to learn.* Do this even if you don't quite get its direct application to what you're doing now. You can only prove your ability to assume the next position on the ladder if you're willing to stretch from where you are.

3. *Try to make yourself a source of information.* Be the person that people turn to in moments of haste when they need an answer.

4. *Get to know the people around you.* And let them get to know the personal side of who you are. Promotions are made based on how well people know you. If two equally qualified people are up for the same job, the person who gets it is the one who's remembered, well-liked, and a known entity.

13

How to Do
What *You* Want

I bet you had visions of skiing condos or beach umbrellas just now, didn't you? Well, if that's what you really want, what are you doing reading *this* book? Grab a vacation guide instead, and go for it! (I was just about to say there are plenty of jobs for waitresses, waiters, and housekeeping in paradise. But come to think of it, there is also a demand for office support in those parts as well. So you might as well keep reading.)

Okay, so let's talk about what you want within the scope of your current job. Financial reward, of course. That goes without saying. How about respect? Upward mobility? Some control over your workday? Clearly defined priorities? Maybe even some anxiety-free hours? The ability to end the day with a sense of mission accomplished, with no ragged ends hanging over into the next day?

As Eliza Doolittle sang in *My Fair Lady,* "Oh, wouldn't it be loverly?" Her vision came true for her, but only after she faced down Professor Higgins, who had his own ideas about how she should spend her time and do her work.

Now I'm going to tell you how to seize control of your day, how to manage *up,* and how to keep your own life in focus. That way you won't lose your career years putting out other people's fires, over and over again, with no upward mobility for you. (I don't know about you, but the last thing I want to be known for is being the best solver of other people's problems.)

Your future starts now.

Oh, wouldn't that be loverly?

First, let's paint a picture of your office circumstances. In this era of doing more with less, I bet you have two, five, maybe even eight people who look to you for assistance. Each has his or her own personality, priorities, and job performance rating to worry about. And although they may not make it obvious (or maybe they do), if push came to real shove, they couldn't care less about each other's workload. *Just as long as theirs gets done first.*

I bet you have a lot of me-firsters on your team. Oh, on a day-to-day basis, they may hide it in favor of building their reputations as team players. That's important for their personal career paths, too.

Now, I also bet that on your team you have at least one person about whom you might think now and then, "Man, what a pain in the rear." This person waltzes into your cubicle, slaps another stack of work in your in-box, apologizes for the last-minute project, says it will only take a minute, gives you a deadline, and waltzes back out. You think, "A minute? Three hours, more likely. And how do I fit it into this tower of priority projects over here?"

You know that's not what your team member is thinking. He or she is thinking, "Hey, I'm finally getting this delegating thing down. Maybe I'm management (executive, entrepreneur) material after all."

So, here you already have a conflict of purpose, don't you? It's only partly about the job at hand. It's also about *their* power plays, *their* résumé building, and *their* job keeping. All those things that have everything to do with *their* careers, but nothing to do with yours.

Notice I use the words *their* and *your*. In these days of teams *their*, *your*, *us*, and *them* are politically incorrect terms. We are all *us*, unless of course *they* are the competition. But if it doesn't really feel that way to you from where you sit, you need to learn not only how join the team, but also how to manage it. Imagine that . . . delegating *up!*

But before giving you this new tool to boost your career, I want to take an old friend away from you—your in-box. You've outgrown that thing. It's cluttering your desk. And it has turned against you. In fact, I wonder if it ever really was your friend.

You two have always been at cross-purposes. Your job is to empty it. Its job is to stay full.

No matter how full or empty it is, it's telling the world bad things about you. If it's full, you look like you're not getting anything done. If it's empty, it looks like you have nothing to do. If it goes full/empty/full/empty/full, it tells the story of your career: a lot of productivity, but no real headway.

Who needs that? Get rid of it.

The best thing it can do for you now is to be conspicuous by its absence. Sooner or later, one of your supervisors is going to come up with a stack of work and say, "Hey, where's your in-box?"

And that will be your chance to tell your team about your new organization management tool—the task log.

Here's how it works:

THE WORK TASK LOG

Like those kitchen gadgets advertised on late night television, this tool does several things at once. It positions you as being extraordinarily cooperative and organized. It takes you out of the energy-draining, time-wasting turf battle over your time. And it consistently ratchets up your career prospects because it keeps an ongoing record of what you've accomplished, what projects you've managed from start to finish, and what tasks it's time for you to delegate down to.

Where the in-box is a one-channel tool designed for a one-channel chain of command, the task log is a multiple-channel organization approach that makes the team members responsible for working out their priorities before they come to you with their requests.

Here's the way it works with the standard in-box: One supervisor comes to you and says, "Here's some work." Then another boss comes to you and says, "Here's some work."

Then a third boss comes to you and says, "Here's some work." Then boss number one comes back and says, "How's my work coming?" Then boss number two comes back and says, "How's my work coming?" Then boss number three comes back and says, "How's my work coming?"

Then, you guessed it, boss number one comes back but is a little more demanding, "What's keeping you? I really need my work today." And we're back on this round-robin where everyone is dumping not only their work on you but also their accumulating pressure and frustration.

And what do you do? You start working harder, harder, harder, faster, faster, faster, making more and more mistakes—and ruining your excellent work record. And what do you know? It gets returned to you the next day to be done over.

Replace the in-box with your task log and the frustrations are over, the interruptions are over, and you pass the job of fighting over your time to the supervisors. If they have any questions about the status of their work, all they have to do is check the log and leave you alone.

I've copied an example of the log on page 181 so that you can refer to it as we review the way it is organized.

First, get a three-ring binder—nothing fancy—and dedicate a spot in your work area for it. A side table is a good idea or the far end of your cubicle. Make it accessible to everyone, but try not to keep it on your immediate work space. That would only invite your supervisors to come up and talk with you about it. And that would defeat its self-serve purpose, wouldn't it?

Fill the binder with lined paper and create seven columns across the page. (The task log is supposed to make life easier for you. You don't want spreadsheet-mania. So keep it simple.) These are the columns and this is how you use them:

1. *Time?* What time did the work come in?

2. *Client?* Who gave you that work? Does the word "client" seem too high-falutin'? Remember that management fash-

ion today is to consider everyone you do work with as a customer or client. So use the term and position yourself as cutting-edge. Eventually, you will be your own client. When you generate your own work—and you will as you grow—you will find your own initials in that column more and more. That's a great sign!

3. *Kind?* What kind of work is this project? A proposal? A budget? A piece of correspondence?

4. *Due?* When must it be finished?

5. *Long?* What time is the job completed and how long did it take you to finish? Indicate with a different color pen if the job was done on time.

6. *Interruptions?* What were the causes?

7. *Result?* What was the outcome? And what ideas do you have for getting the job done better the next time? The suggestion portion may be blank for many projects that go well, but there will be that space set aside for those, shall we say, learning experiences.

Right now, this may seem like extra work for you. And maybe at the start, it will be. But, as you will see in Chapter 14, once you and your team members get accustomed to using the task log, the little extra effort you invest at this early stage will pay huge dividends within days. It will put you in the position of attracting more interesting projects, and cultivating those management and creative skills that will skyrocket your career.

In the next chapter, I'll show you how.

14

How to Make the Task Log Work for You

Okay, so now you have this binder with all these columns. What good is it going to do you? It will do wonders, provided that you focus on ways to maximize its benefits. Here's just a sampling of its advantages. The binder will help you:

- Control the work flow.
- Manage your own workday and career.
- Make your supervisors accountable for their own projects and negotiate the scheduling priorities with each other, rather than bringing you into the conflict.
- Remember projects that will later position you for significant promotions.
- Identify and delegate repetitive tasks that are perhaps best handled by other, less-seasoned assistants. (Remember that the assignment which is a been-there-done-that nuisance for you might be *just* the opportunity a newcomer needs to boost his or her career to the next level. It's a good thing to delegate.)

So let's see how the task log works. You'll see that the task log in this book covers three days.

It's 8 o'clock in the morning on Day One. Mary Smith is one of your team members. She brings you an assignment and one of you signs it in. (Gradually, you should encourage your supervisors to sign in their own work so they start getting in the habit of using the log before interrupting you.) Under the *Kind?* column, she writes "proposal," and she wants it done by 2:00 P.M. Fair enough.

You eventually take two and a half hours to do it. And while you were at it, you also made five photocopies down the hall and sent two faxes. You have no suggestions because things went smoothly.

In the meantime, at 8:15 A.M. Last-Minute Bob Smith comes along and enters a budget to be completed by 2:30 P.M. But he looks at the log and notices that Mary's job would compete for your time. What does he say? "I've got to have it! Mine is more important. Mine is revenue producing."

"Talk to Mary," is all you have to say.

And Mary, whose priority is her project but who also has an investment in team cohesiveness, tells him a) no and b) if it's that important log it in the night before or earlier in the morning. Whether the conversation becomes a fight or a quiet negotiation, you're out of it. You're serenely down the hall working on Mary's proposal. And your time is being put to good—and appropriate—use.

So, the next morning rolls around, and what do you know? Bob's came in early for once and logged his project in at 7:45 A.M.

Well, maybe. This is a learning experience that might take some time for everyone.

On Day Two, you have also written down an appointment with the copy machine service contractor. But the service contractor doesn't show up, so you write "canceled by contractor" in the Results box. On Day Three you receive an unscheduled visit from another copy machine service provider. He tells you the previous contractor is out of business and he has taken over the accounts. But, he tells you with a sincere look, his service is an upgrade over the one you've previously contracted for. Therefore, to keep the contract in force, your company must pay a premium. Just a nominal charge, say $1,500 extra a year.

"Now wait just a minute," you say. You know that this guy is trying to pull a fast one. So you stand your ground, and make a not-so-vague reference to checking with your firm's legal counsel. Funny how quickly people will back down when they know they're outsmarted. Your contract is honored, and you've saved your department a pot of cash.

So how do you make that success work for you? Write it down on your task log. The time this guy barged in unannounced, how much time he wasted, and the results. What are the results exactly? That you told him off? Well, maybe that was the most satisfying part. But the result that is the most meaningful to the company is that *you just saved it $1,500 a year.*

Underscore that particular notation in *green* (for money). Also write in SAM, for "see attached memo." In your memo, briefly summarize what happened, what was said, how you handled it, and why.

The "why" is particularly important, because it will help you build your future. For instance, maybe you knew your company's rights on service contracts because you just happened to have taken a night course in commercial law. On your own dime, for that matter. Maybe your company isn't as committed as it should be to educating its support staff. And now you can demonstrate in a tangible way exactly how valuable education is throughout all ranks. And you just might get your tuition covered from now on.

Don't underestimate the value of green. Every department in almost every company today is under incredible pressure to justify its existence by its impact on the company's bottom line. Every time you save the company money or make the company money, make sure you record it in your task log. That way you will remember even the smallest incident when your performance appraisal comes up.

Oh, you might think that each incident is so big that there's no way you'll forget it when the time comes to report on your performance. Or you might think the incident is so small that it's not worth remembering at all. That might be true. But I know what it's like to call up information under pressure. It can be done, but the rich detail gets lost when the brain is scrambling to remember. And it's that rich detail, as it adds up day after day of even the smallest successes, that will position you for the next promotion.

So underline those successes in green. Make it your objective to fill your task log with green, green, and more green. Be sure to note the pace with which your green is piling up. For instance, maybe in the beginning of your task log there are not be many incidences that call for green. But as the weeks and months fly by, look for more and more ways you can prove your profitability and record them. Then during your performance appraisal you can show not only profitability but also improvement.

Blue is the second career-building color. Every time you initiate your own project, underline that in blue in your task log. The more work you do that's your own, the less you will have to do that belongs to others. Develop your own projects that support the overall team objectives: newsletters, contact databases, vendor research, and conference planning. Look at what your other team members are doing and see which of their tasks you might volunteer to handle for them. In other words, help *them* move up their own career tracks. The space they leave empty as they rise in their own ambitions is a space they can show you how to fill. Voilà! Up you go.

As you move up, you'll have to leave tasks behind. Graduate yourself and mark your upward mobility in *yellow.* That's the color I want you to use to underline tasks that are either repetitive or that can be delegated to others. These are nowhere tasks. And sure, we all have them. *I* still have them. But many of those yellow tasks you can lose. But first you have to get in the habit of spotting them.

Still typing everyone's correspondence, even though they have their own computers and word processing software? Still standing at the copy machine? Still taking shifts at the reception desk? Has it gotten to the point where you can't take on that fascinating new assignment (producing a company newsletter, for instance, or gathering information to support the purchase of a new high-speed, high-volume copier) because you don't have time?

Yellow tasks are your future-blockers. Mark them in yellow. But don't do anything about them just yet. Simply watch what pattern emerges over the next several weeks or months. And then make a list of what they are and how long you have been doing them. Decide which ones you want to keep and which ones you'd like to pass on.

Does it feel as if you're just shrugging off the junk work? Feel guilty? Don't. These are tasks that opened doors for you. Now it's your turn to help open doors for others coming up after you. It's like the old clothes in your closet. They're still wearable, but you've outgrown their style. But there's someone out there who would really appreciate that old suit of yours that's still in good shape. It's just what they need to look presentable for their first job interview. Hold on tight to it, and no one wears it. Let it go, and you're helping someone else come up the ranks. Same goes for some of your old tasks.

Offer to train the next person, and you can put training on your task log. There! You have something else to underline in blue.

Not quite convinced? Remember what you learned about colors in elementary school. Yellow and blue make green. Combine the blue of your initiative with the yellow of getting rid of your outgrown tasks, and you've made green. Green for the company. By training a fellow employee just a step or two behind you, you are saving the company money in recruitment and training because that employee, seeing a future with the firm, will stay. If the employee left looking for, well, greener pastures elsewhere, your company would have to spend money looking for and training the replacement.

And you've made green for yourself. With "trainer" now on your résumé, you've increased the value of your own potential and abilities within the firm. That will turn into bucks, whether your company gives you a raise or whether you spruce up your résumé and start shopping the job market.

Use it regularly and the task log can change your life. The task log is your "shine utility." You know how your computer has a utilities folder that helps the computer get its job done? Well, your "shine utility" helps you keep track of how well you get *your* job done. And it's a record of the great ideas and initiatives you've taken to get the job done better, faster, and cheaper.

Better, faster, and cheaper. Companies like that. Those are the three ingredients in the profit recipe. And when you show that you are a key contributor to its profit potential, you're on your way to the next level in your career.

15

How to Get What You Need

This chapter is going to require just a little bit of math. But stick with me. I promise it won't be hard, and the results will help you get just about any piece of office equipment you want. Maybe even free parking if you can apply this new principle to your commuting needs. Once you have this formula down, you can use it to make your life much easier, less frustrating, more productive, and more valuable.

Remember that principle that the cheesier your office space is, the lower your salary probably is as well? The reverse is frequently also true. The nicer the space, the higher your status. You can wait for that high status to get the better equipment. And you could wait forever.

Get the better equipment first, and watch your status skyrocket!

Let's use my personal bugaboo as an example of what I mean: copy machines. I hated them when I was a secretary, and I still hate copy machines even though I'm no longer working in a large company. Here's a scenario I know you're familiar with. You've got a big document to copy and plenty of other tasks logged in on your task log. But you've got to get this thing copied.

So you find someone to agree to take the phone calls that come in while you're away from the desk. That's time-consuming. Then you walk down the hall to the group's copy machine. That's time-consuming. Since it's being shared by the entire department, of course, there's someone already at the machine. So you stand in line. How time-consuming is that?

Then you have to switch paper trays. Then the machine jams or runs out of toner. Then someone comes up behind you and says, "I just have a . . ." Oh, you know what's next: ". . . a couple of pages. Can I sneak in for just a minute?" "Sure," you say. You're a team member, right? You want to be cooperative. So you stand aside. And the machine jams on that person. "Rats," says the interloper, who then walks away looking for a working machine—leaving you to unjam the jam.

How many priorities did you just respond to in that scenario besides your own? Way too many, I'd say. From the moment you start looking around for someone to take the incoming calls, you've put your career in the hands of a long line of people who really couldn't care less.

How about a copy machine of your very own? Here is how you get it: by producing a cost-benefit analysis.

Sounds horrible, doesn't it? Cost-benefit analysis. You're probably thinking, "If I wanted to learn about cost-benefit analyses I would have gotten my MBA."

I'm not expecting you to warm up to the term, but just follow along and you'll see how surprisingly easy it is. And think about how awful the copy machine experience is. Week after week of that kind of frustration can be traded in for just a few minutes of math. Pretty good deal, if you ask me.

You know what? We just did a cost-benefit analysis! Week after week of frustration versus a few minutes of math. That's a cost-benefit analysis. See? And you didn't even feel it.

Okay, let's get down to one that you can actually present to your supervisors. And you might actually net yourself your very own copy machine. Here's how it goes:

Remember the acronym SAM ("see attached memo")? You want to present your case for analysis attached to a log entry that was particularly grueling. It took forever, for instance, to return to that pressing proposal, because you couldn't give up your place in line to copy that not-so-pressing budget job. Or the senior vice president tried to reach your supervisor repeatedly during that time but the phone just rang and rang and rang, because you were wasting precious minutes of your life standing in the copy line. In other words, pick an event in which your supervisor could see how he or she was also negatively affected by your absence from your desk.

Now, compose a memo that is unmistakably well-reasoned, smart, and budget-conscious. This is a memo that will position you not as a complainer but as a problem solver:

> You'll see by this log entry that x happened because of my absence from my desk. I was at the copy machine for x minutes. These avoidable factors contributed to delaying my return: [*Outline what happened, but don't go into too much detail or you'll sound whiney*]. I have figured out a way we can avoid this costly event in the future.
>
> I spend an average of x minutes away from my desk every day while I'm making copies. Multiply that by $4\frac{1}{3}$ weeks a month, and multiply that by 12 months a year. That adds up to x hours away from my desk. At my hourly rate of $\$x$, my trips to the copy machine are costing us [*always us, you're a member of the team, remember*] $\$x,xxx$ a year for this function. Additionally, this function presents an added cost to the company because it prevents me from performing other tasks at the same time.
>
> A copier dedicated to my workstation would allow me to perform other duties while copying documents. One that meets our quality standards is currently available for $\$xxx.xx$. It would pay for itself in x weeks.

That's easy. All you have to do is know your hourly rate and be able to multiply (or use a calculator, which is my favorite way to go).

By using the cost-benefit analysis you boost your career in several ways:

• You reinforce your image as a problem solver, not a complainer.

• You remind your supervisors that your top priority is their interests, not keeping your frustration level down to a minimum. (That's a secret we'll just keep to ourselves.)

• You stay on top of the market by knowing how much important equipment costs. And, if company budget does not include a photocopier (which the bean counters might have considered a major expense but your savvy shopping has shown otherwise), appeal to the renegade that beats in the heart of everyone. Divide the cost of the copier by the number of team members you have, put a little conspiratorial gleam in your eye, and then ask each one to add her share to the fund to buy a team copy machine. You can even call it the Copy Pot!

Make it fun and humorous. But remember that you're responding to a very serious obligation you have to your employer. As the administrative honcho, it's your job to initiate efficient work processes. And that includes knowing how much—or in this case how little—things cost. Go up to your bosses and say "I want a copy machine," and visions of $10,000 come to mind.

But go up to your bosses and say "I have found a way to save the company $x a month, and it only costs $x one time," and you'll get an entirely positive response.

Maybe even a "Good thinking! Thanks!"

A successful cost-benefit analysis calls for using both a blue and green marker on your task log.

And that will reap even more dividends come performance appraisal time.

That's all there is to a cost-benefit analysis. Not so bad, is it? Especially when you consider the returns.

─────── 16 ───────

EXPAND YOUR CIRCLE

OF INFLUENCE

There's been a lot of fuss over networking for the last five to ten years. Have you noticed? Maybe it has to do with the millions of middle managers who have found themselves downsized out of a job. All of a sudden they started to realize, "Uh oh, maybe I should have kept up my contacts." Well, yes.

I've never been a big fan of the word "networking," but I'm wild about "positioning." I'd like you to think about *positioning* yourself in your company. This is a marketing term, the process that goes along with branding. For instance, you're in the market for a car. You want one that is easy and unpretentious to own; a car whose reputation says, "Built with pride and dignity by American hands." Would you buy a Saturn or a Mercedes? Or you want a car that is a rolling lap of luxury, one that speaks of a timeless tradition of precision and elegance. Would you buy a Saturn or a Mercedes?

The answers are obvious. And I haven't mentioned anything about the engine, the mechanics, the service records, or even the price of each car. But we agree which one is which. Companies spend hundreds of thousands of dollars distinguishing themselves from each other. As they should, since the automotive industry is a high-stakes deal.

You don't have to spend any money at all. And you really don't have to worry about getting confused with the assistant next door. The difference in education, skills, attitude, and appearance does all that for you. But what you *do* want to achieve is first-place position in your colleagues' minds. So when an opportunity comes along that needs your package of skills, you are everyone's first choice for the job.

How do I want you to position yourself? As a resourceful, responsible professional who can take a project from beginning to end; someone who gets his or her phone calls returned; someone who makes it happen (no matter what "it" is). Can you do that? Of course. Here's how: Build your own team—a team of sponsors.

SPONSORS VS. MENTORS

We've all heard of mentors, maybe you even have one or two. (And I certainly hope you *are* one to someone else coming up behind you.) These are individuals who stand by to offer you advice on career moves and ideas on how to handle a sensitive situation. They're the ones who can help you see new ways to transform office politics into *opportunities to prevail.* Mentors are good to have no matter where you are in your career. But the mentor relationship is a one-way street. Someone is mentoring you, or you're mentoring someone else. A reciprocal mentorship is rare.

You'll find sponsors everywhere in the organizational chart. These are the people who help you tap into the entire company's resources to far exceed the expectations of your team—and astonish everyone again and again! Your sponsors will help you find new employees for your team, market your team's projects, and save your team money. Every time your sponsors get involved, it's a guaranteed green or blue entry in your task log.

So how do you recruit your sponsors? Look at the areas within your organization that overlap what you do, or areas through which you source things out. The three areas are purchasing, marketing, and finance. You need to get to know your counterparts in those departments. I'm not particularly suggesting that you become *friends* with them. But you do want to be warm acquaintances with them. You want them to know your name and you want to know theirs.

You're expanding your circle of influence, very much like students in college do when they join fraternities and sororities. Do you think a Kappa Beta Kappa sister in a petroleum company ignores a phone message from another Kappy sister just because she works in a greeting card company and they don't know each other? Absolutely not. They have a commonality established, and they haven't even met! That phone call gets answered.

So, since you have the advantage of reading this book, it's up to you to establish the commonalities among your counterparts in these important departments. Find out those who do what you do in each department, call them up, and invite them to lunch. Simple as that.

Oh, no, you're thinking. Not so simple. These people don't know me, and they'll be suspicious. What's up my sleeve? Am I trying to pull a fast one? This is how you can put it:

> I'm reading this fantastic book called *Will the* Real *Boss Please Stand Up?* It's about getting ahead for office professionals, and it recommends we get together and compare notes on how we can help each other out. So I thought it would be a good idea to start a monthly lunch of just us so we can keep each other up-to-date on what we're doing and what we need. I'm also inviting Susan, John, and Paula. Which day would be best for you?

Emphasize that what you want to do is build a team of colleagues for mutual help. You're not looking for another job, and you're certainly not looking to take his or her job. You just want to put into place a mechanism for reciprocating help. That could someday mean an extra pair of friendly hands during a production crunch, or a recommendation for just the right vendor when you need to outsource a project. (It's said you're only as good as your contacts. I'd like to improve on that: You're only as good as your contacts' contacts.)

This is how you start getting people to look out for you and you to look out for them.

So let's break this little group down in parts. Why, for instance, should purchasing be in the group? Say your boss comes out of his office and says, "We need a fax machine this year." Now what he's really just said is, "Go into the market-place, source it out, come back with recommendations, and then tell me how we're going to fund it."

That's a big order. So what's your first step? You can start with the library. That's twenty minutes there and twenty minutes back, plus three hours spent in the library, which nets you a listing of twenty-two manufacturers and dealers and a *Consumer Reports* article about the top six machines. That's a whole afternoon down the drain.

Or you can hit the Internet and do your research online. But if you're doing that at your desk, you'll be constantly interrupted with other tasks and ringing telephones. Or you can go through past issues of business magazines and clip the advertisements. Do you have the last twelve issues of *Fortune* within reach? I didn't think so.

One quick call to the purchasing department will streamline the process to just a few minutes. Since their job is to buy office equipment and supplies, they've probably already done the research on which fax machine is the best choice for your level of output. Additionally, they may also have a volume-purchase relationship with a vendor, so you won't have to pay retail.

So you want to be able to pick up the phone and ask, "Hi Paula, what do you know about fax equipment?" or "Has anybody else in the company recently purchased a fax machine? Who was it? I want to talk with them."

Purchasing is an obvious match with your department. What about finance? What can the accountants do for you? Say that fax isn't budgeted for. As much as you need it, the money just doesn't seem to be there. If you're friendly with someone in the finance department, all you have to do is pick up the phone. The two of you can strategize ways to market your purchase decision in such a way that it makes financial sense.

Remember Radar O'Reilly in *M*A*S*H* and how he could magically make badly needed surgical equipment, medicines, and furniture appear? That can be you, known for your resourcefulness and ability to make things happen when lesser mortals sigh and say, "No way, it can't be done."

So what can marketing do for you? Marketing is your company's future. They know six, twelve, eighteen months into the future, before anyone else does, which new products are slated to be rolled out, who the new customer populations will be, and which new skills will be needed within the company. You want to make sure you know ahead of time what's coming down the pike. Wait and learn it with everybody else, and you're going to be in a reactive mode—not the *proactive* mode you always want to be positioned in. As an anticipatory assistant with a vision for future developments, you can give your supervisors an information edge over everyone else in the entire company.

Be the one to inform your department of what the future looks like, and you'll be the one to help drive your department toward that future. You'll also be the one other departments want to recruit by dangling all sorts of delightful enticements to attract you.

──────── PROFILE ────────

José Rego
Project Coordinator
Arquitectonica International Corp.
Miami, FL

The first job I had in Miami was as a secretary for an interior contractor company. I was told, "You're here to type, do correspondence, and answer phones." Then an attorney hired me for my clerical and secretarial skills. He gave me the training I needed to be a good legal secretary. That was extremely beneficial to me. It was like going to school for free. And I worked with him for eight years.

During this time people tended to emphasize what I was lacking rather than what skills and talents I was performing with. Egos shine by putting other people down. And when you're in the legal field, you dealing with extremely big egos. But you can't do anything about what they are. You can only do something about yourself.

I decided I didn't want to work in a legal career anymore. Unless you're a paralegal, it's hard to get the respect and consideration that really should be due you. And I wanted to get more responsibility.

So I went to work at a hotel management firm, taking on all the administrative responsibilities and handling the local bank account. This is what I needed to do and what I liked to do, taking ownership of things, seeing things through from beginning to end.

I believe in the field of administrative support. I will be the one to support your needs and represent you and your business to the outside world. I see the value in this role in business. My current employment has proven that to me.

Arquitectonica is an international company that's involved with the expansion of the Miami International Airport. I came to them when they announced that they needed someone with light bookkeeping, light supervisory, and heavy administrative experience. There's a lot of detail in my job: the administrative aspects of the projects they're working on, and dealing with outside consultants and vendors directly. More often than not, people will contact me rather than deal with the architects themselves.

I designed it that way to give the architects more time to do what they do, which is design.

Finding a job that gives you this kind of autonomy isn't impossible. But you do need to know what to look for. You also need a little bit of luck in finding people who have the ability to let go and say, "Yes. Here, take ownership."

When I am looking for a new job, I look for a corporation that has been established for some time. I study its industry to try to identify its trends and future prospects for growth. And I want to work with someone who communicates, someone who takes the time to inform me, to give me an understanding of the company's history, its principles, even its future. I think it's also important to ask the interviewer what the growth opportunities are.

Nobody ever asks me if I've got a "girl's job." I personally do not see it that way. I have found a lot of people are very comfortable working with male assistants. I have found it rewarding, and people trust me very much. That's what matters.

My advice is:

1. *Stay informed.* Read the industry magazines, as well as publications related to administrative support.

2. *Learn to market yourself internally and externally.* Let people know what you are accomplishing and what more you can do. Learn to blow your own horn. That's where your security will come from.

3. *Be very aware of what your strengths are and what your weaknesses are.* The times when you have to confront your weaknesses could become very hazardous. If you already know you're weak in an area, you can build up your strength and knowledge there.

17

THE CIRCLES OUTSIDE
YOUR SPHERE

Your circles of influence extend far beyond the internal corporate sponsors we just talked about. Because you're serious about your career, you must position yourself as a familiar face in your business community. I know that's not easy to do, especially when you have a full workload and a family that waits for you at home. One more thing to do? Could that possibly be the straw that breaks the camel's back?

I sure hope not. If you're feeling overwhelmed by everything you already have to do, take the following advice a little bit at a time. Sure, you can go whole hog and join all sorts of committees and take on tons of new responsibility . . . if you want to. But what I'd rather suggest is that you take it a little bit at a time. It's like going to the gym and learning to lift weights. Start slow and gradually build up your skills and capacity to do even more.

Feeling better? Great. Let's get started.

Nested inside your job are at least three career tracks. By the time we're done here, you should be ready to make a name for yourself in all these tracks.

First (but not necessarily foremost), you are an administrative professional. Whatever your title may be (secretary, administrative assistant, or executive assistant, for example), your profession is represented by the organization Professional Secretaries International (PSI), which is based in Kansas City, Missouri. This group is a must-join for you. Even if your ambition is to graduate yourself beyond this kind of career,

PSI gives you a great foundation for leveraging the skills you already have.

PSI also offers a certification program that will enhance your standing as a professional within your company. The certified professional secretary designation (or CPS) is an achievement to be proud of. It's a credential that makes your résumé stand out from those of all the other applicants who are inexperienced enough to think that your profession is a snap. It tells recruiters that you take your career and yourself extremely seriously—and that you're dedicated to growing your professional stature.

You don't have to be a member of PSI to be eligible to take the certification exam. It is given twice a year, in May and November, at most community colleges throughout the country. (When you call for information, make sure you pronounce the *S* in CPS *very* carefully. The receptionist might think you're asking about the CPA exam and give you the wrong date!)

You will be tested on material that you already know thoroughly—the skills you practice everyday on the job. So you *will* pass the exam. You *will* possess that CPS designation. And, you know what? You will also receive college credits.

You can let those credits go ignored. Or you can march them to your college's admissions office and ask, "How do I get a degree?" Colleges from coast to coast are making it easier for adults to return to formal education and get their degrees, capitalizing on the life experiences they've accumulated, from their last day of school as children and to their first day back at school as adults.

Think that's too much? I know one man who has three children under age 6. He's forty-five years old, and only had a high school degree until he returned to college two years ago. His major is Chinese relations, and he has to be able to speak Chinese almost fluently as a graduation requirement. Imagine learning Chinese at age 45. And he's making the dean's list!

He started out as a secretary.

By the way, in case you have test anxiety, like me, let me reassure you right now that the colleges that offer the CPS test also offer a refresher course. It takes you through a simulated exam, so you will get an idea of what some of the questions will be like.

Once you achieve the CPS, market your new achievement as much as you can.

1. *Tell the human resources department that you have added that credential to your résumé.* Ask them to include this achievement in your personal file so that it will be taken into account when considering you for a raise or promotion.

2. *Have your employer print a new set of business cards with the CPS designation after your name.* If your company doesn't print business cards for its administrative professionals, have your own cards printed up at your local quick copy service. If you print your own, the cards are unofficial as far as your employer is concerned. You won't be able to use the company logo, but you *can* indicate which company you work for. Include your business cards in all your professional correspondence (if it's a company-printed card, include the card in official correspondence). And be prepared to distribute your cards to the many new people you will meet as you expand your external spheres of influence.

3. *Make sure your company announces your achievement in its employee communications,* whether it's an intranet or internal newsletter.

As you develop your career as an administrative professional, you may also develop a name for yourself within your employer's profession or industry. Thousands of trade and professional associations represent every business you can think of. Your company's business is bound to have a representative group. If you live in a large urban area, the chances are also excellent that the association has a local chapter. If you live in your state's capital, your local chapter is also the state chapter, with a lot of added responsibilities, such as political lobbying and membership information and training.

No matter what level your local chapter represents, get active in that group as quickly as you can. This is the one professional environment that is probably open to all who earn their living in the field. And no one is as interested in your rank on the employer's organization chart as they are in your eagerness to serve the association.

These kinds of groups have committees galore, from public relations to legislative affairs. This is your chance to volunteer for projects that will put you in the limelight, and earn you recognition that could result in a promotion or a new job altogether. The contacts you make in these groups are lifetime contacts that could see you through retirement.

Among the members of this group, you will have access to leaders throughout all levels of other related businesses, including vendors who will offer association members special deals on their products and services. If you think it's valuable being friendly with your colleagues, wait until you experience the power of reaching for the membership directory, selecting the name of a high-powered fellow member, and calling that person to introduce yourself.

You will be the one who makes things happen for your team. Better stock up on those green and blue pens.

The third track is your home community's economic development organization. That's your local chamber of commerce or trade council. These groups usually host monthly networking meetings after hours. That's an okay place to start. But limit yourself to those events and you'll soon be pegged as someone on the make—doing nothing much more than looking for a new job or a new business opportunity.

Real value, once again, comes from volunteering on projects and committees. Some groups sponsor a Habitat for Humanity home-building project. Some launch an annual familiarization trip in which they host visiting site selectors from corporations thinking about relocating to the area. Once again, all these projects are high-visibility events that are completely indifferent to corporate rank or social status. You might find yourself installing a window frame with the CEO of your local hospital, or designing a welcome brochure with the head of the area's largest advertising firm.

Casual conversation. Lucky happenstance. Brilliant careers are built on these marvelous twists of fate.

Be active on one of these three tracks, or get involved in all of them. Whatever you choose, invest yourself in their activities and be a regular at their meetings and functions.

1. *Get information.* You know the old saw: Let other people do the talking, then they'll find you absolutely fascinating. And they'll remember you for being absolutely fascinating. And you'll remember them for that little tidbit of advice, wisdom, or inside information that could boost your career to the next level.

2. *Ask for advice or help.* I know a very successful lobbyist in Washington, D.C., who says this about making friends: "The best way to gain an ally is not by doing that person a favor. It's by asking that person for a favor." Recruit people to your mission (preferably a mission that benefits others), and you have created a cadre of supporters who are personally invested in your success. You've also flattered them, making them feel very rich and wise indeed for having the resources that are useful to you. And how savvy you must be for noticing them and what they can offer.

3. *Remember to help others.* Start looking out for other people. Start matching the opportunities that come your way with just the right people. When you start looking out for other people, other people will start looking out for you.

4. *Tune into the WOM frequency.* Word of mouth. Be there at the meetings, be there at all the social functions. The right person will spot you across a crowded room, and the sight of you might spark a connection in this person's mind. And the next thing you know, you've got a name and phone number that will change your life.

18

Office Politics Is
Your Opportunity to
Prevail

You probably already know this: Nothing will make the phone ring faster than the simple act of settling down to concentrate on a project.

Over the past four days, I have sat down in this chair at least ten times to start working on this chapter. And every time I poise my fingers over the computer keyboard, the phone rings. Or there's a knock on the door. Or a client moves a proposal deadline ahead seventy-two hours. A board of directors that I serve on is in a twist over the wording of new by-laws. The neighborhood association is having its biannual meeting, and one of the agitators is trying to recruit me to their side. And . . . and . . . and . . . and. It never ends!

"Hmm," I say to myself, "this is annoying. And it's slowing down my productivity."

Maybe I can use this somehow. I can write a chapter on how irritating it is to be interrupted. No, where's the news there? You can write volumes on that one, I'm sure. No, I think I'll use it to demonstrate that no matter who you are or what your office situation is, you are always at the mercy of OPP, or other people's priorities, which is the source of that most dreadful career reality—office politics.

I can't escape them, and I mostly work alone. Certainly *you* can't escape them. So maybe we can figure this one out together. And as always, our mission here is to figure out ways we can assume our own power and approach the problem as an architect of the changes we choose for ourselves—not as a victim of the changes others are trying to make to suit their own priorities.

As an office professional you are subject to being a key player in other people's priorities. You're interrupted all day long by people who want access to what you have and whom you represent. If you aren't able to size up a political power play early in the game, you will find that your own effectiveness is compromised, your time is wasted, your reputation is ruined, and you're sucked into a tempest that someone else has cooked up. There is absolutely no upside for you in this scenario.

But learn to identify the hidden agendas early and you'll become a valuable advisor to your supervisor and an early warning system that can save a company or project. You'll be that much more indispensable as you demonstrate that no matter how hard the winds blow around you, you can keep a steady, firm hand on the direction of your department. Office politics can actually be turned around to make you shine in the eyes of valued supervisors who will soon open the next door leading to your future.

This is the chance to reframe our natural negative reaction to office politics into a positive phenomenon. Let's learn to look at office politics instead as "opportunities to prevail."

We'd better get cracking. It's almost 8:30 on a Sunday morning and the phone is going to ring any second. I just know it.

Why should we even have office politics? You'd think that by now civilization and theories of organizational development, at least, would have figured out a way to boil that out of the business soup. Isn't moving in fast-forward hard enough without having to look over your shoulder at the same time? Isn't there enough to do in a single day without getting caught up in someone else's petty schemes and paranoias? It's very inefficient to be a character in a power play that you didn't write.

Actually, you're already a master at office politics on a

basic level. Do you have a job? Do you come to work on time every day? Do you meet your deadlines? Do you accept your paycheck without loudly demanding every time that it should be more? That's politics. You're already playing the game: Having successfully followed the rules of playing to the hiring manager, you are now doing what the boss wants, the way he or she wants it. In return, you get a previously agreed upon sum of money. In political circles, that's called *quid pro quo* . . . this for that. The political bargain you've struck is a legitimate one: "I'll be dependable and productive. In return, you be reasonable and pay me what we agreed upon." This for that. *Quid pro quo.*

That wasn't so bad, was it? The terms are clear, there are no hidden agendas, and, presumably, it's a win/win situation for both of you. Both sides make choices based on a full disclosure of the facts. That may not be the sneaky context we usually associate with office politics, but it's still office politics. So give yourself credit for what you already know.

Office politics takes on a bad smell when harmful manipulations begin to seep into relationships. Why do people get involved in harmful interactions in the office? Several reasons. But it usually comes right down to ego and fear.

COMMUNICATION BREAKDOWNS

PEOPLE ARE AFRAID THEY'RE GOING TO LOSE THEIR JOBS

All around you people are jockeying for a secure position. You're surrounded by deserted offices and cubicles. Maybe your staff directory is only two months old, but a huge percentage of its listings have already been laid off. Or maybe your company is just fine, but the major employer down the street has just shrugged off thousand of workers. Even though today's newspapers are tending toward stories about companies beefing up their ranks again, employees know that job security—heck, job *success*—might forever be merely a matter of being the last one standing.

To be the last one standing means that everyone else has to fall. That's a climate for cutthroat politics if I ever saw one.

THERE'S A LACK OF CLEARLY STATED STANDARDS OF PERFORMANCE AND COMPANY MISSION

When the rules are unclear, employees will make them up as they go along. And you only need one cunning power monger to set up a tense environment of doubt and mistrust. You think you might know who it is: It's probably that guy who dresses just like the boss and laughs at all his stupid jokes. Could be. But I submit he's just the one doing it badly. There might be someone else close to you this very minute . . . someone you've been confiding in.

SOME MANAGERS THINK EMPLOYEE RIVALRY IS A GOOD MOTIVATION TECHNIQUE

It amazes me to think that there are still those dinosaurs on the planet, running businesses and ruining people's lives. But, in fact, there are still those who enjoy watching the aftermath of the havoc they wreak over their own staff. Personally I find this kind of environment demoralizing, and it drains my energy and creativity. You might be like me, or you might like life on this kind of edge. If your productivity is affected one way or the other by the atmosphere set up by the boss, be sure to ask prospective supervisors what their motivation philosophy is. If their approach is 180 degrees different from yours, don't even second-guess your ability to find happiness on that job. Stand up, extend your hand, say "thank you very much for your time," and get out of there as fast as you can.

EVERYONE HAS BUTTONS TO PUSH

When you hold a power position—and don't think you don't—you have something someone else wants. In your case, it's probably access and influence. Instead of coming right up and asking you for it, some colleagues will, in effect, mug you for it. They'll size you up and figure out what will get you on their side. For me, there's nothing like a good compliment to get me motivated to go that extra mile for someone. For others, it's fearful intimidation.

The office muggers are efficient and effective at pushing buttons. It's as if there were a step-by-step manual for evil manipulation out there, available only in stores where books for bad guys are sold. It's not so easy to spot it being done on yourself (see the next section for a few ideas). But you've probably watched an expert play a supervisor or a colleague like a fiddle. Haven't you wondered, "Why don't they get what's being done to them?" There might be someone wondering the same thing about you.

YOUR ROLE IN SOMEONE ELSE'S GAME

It's easy for someone in your position to get caught up in someone else's play for power. Get the reputation as an easy mark, and your efforts and productivity will take a sharp nosedive. And maybe even your loyalties will be called into question as the wrong people gain access to your supervisor. You'll just be standing there flabbergasted, wondering "What did I do?"

What you might have done was not fully appreciate the extent of your true power. Power? You? Yes, you. As you will soon discover by reading get-ahead books written for middle managers and executives, you will discover that Rule Number 1 for power gathering is "Get chummy with the secretary."

You probably already see yourself as the gatekeeper to your supervisor's day. But do you really understand how much power you wield as far as the outside world is concerned? In his excellent book *Winning Office Politics*, Andrew DuBrin dedicates an entire chapter to cultivating relationships with support staff. The very first piece of advice in his chapter

"Planning Your Political Campaign" is, "Get information from secretaries and administrative assistants." He writes:

> Assistants . . . are an important information hub. They are often aware of pending organizational changes that could lead to demotions or promotions; they can identify the powerful people in the organizations; and they know who their immediate boss likes and dislikes. Assistants who think positively of you will often share their perceptions with powerful people. . . .

Did you know you had that kind of clout? Well, you do now.

How to Tell If You're Being Used

Being used is not always a bad thing. In fact, we're paid to be used for the time and skills we've agreed to market. But you need to be aware of all the ambitious colleagues, middle managers, and executives who have read those career books and now have you in their sights.

Here are some surefire heads-up signals that you are being used as a pawn:

A Change in Behavior

Suddenly someone is very nice to you. Normally that person wouldn't even give you change for a soda. Now he or she just loves your new haircut, your dress, the way you keep your desk tidy, or the way you answer the phone. Or maybe there's a plate of donuts waiting for you. He'll use any excuse to butter you up. Accept the compliments and gifts with grace. And smile to yourself when he comes around again with a little more butter. He may think he's playing you for a sucker. He doesn't need to know you're wise to him. Plus, the donuts are delicious.

STUPID QUESTIONS

You may suddenly find yourself being asked inconsequential questions, some vaguely worded query designed to indirectly reveal your boss's schedule or priorities. These questions serve two purposes: They can be used as ice breakers or puzzle pieces. As ice breakers they warm you up, as you answer one question after another, before finally setting you up to deliver the answer to the Big Question. Before you know it, you've just given away the store. Or if they're used as puzzle pieces, you never answer the Big Question, but you've answered all the little ones around it. With enough of these puzzle pieces fitting together, it's a simple matter to deduce the answer to the Big Question.

There's a third way to use stupid questions, a technique I've seen used by reporters. Sometimes reporters will intentionally ask questions based on obviously mistaken assumptions. They're playing on human nature, which just can't resist the chance to correct a falsehood. And then you're off and yakking away, giving out all sorts of information that compromises your department's interests.

EVIDENCE OF NIGHT VISITORS

Your Rolodex, calendar, and interoffice memos are among your most valuable assets. And night visitors don't only come in the night. Even in the middle of the morning, a few moments away from your desk with the wrong file open is the ticket into your department's security and your supervisor's secrets. Protect your computer files with a password that only you—and perhaps your supervisor—know. Lock up your other files, along with a backup disk of the day's work, in a secure drawer before you leave at night.

YOU'RE ASKED TO TAKE SIDES

One of your greatest strengths as an office professional is the ability to share with and support your peers. This is a great way to stay current on company trends, get inside insights on new hires, and learn what new software is available to take the load off just a little more. This is state-of-the-art networking. But if you suddenly find yourself ready to take up someone else's battle, even when there is no obvious benefit to you or your boss, this is your warning signal that you've been suckered. Get off that battleground quick. And, if necessary, come clean with your boss that you inadvertently stumbled onto a problem.

SHOULD YOU TELL THE BOSS?

Yes. Just as you are the world's gateway to your supervisor, you are also your supervisor's window on the world. More often than not, you know who wants your boss's time long before he or she does. You may also have advance notice that there's intrigue in the wind.

You know your boss's rhythms better than anyone. Perhaps he or she prefers a weekly update. Perhaps your supervisor wants to know everything as soon as you know it.

It's your responsibility to find out exactly how he or she wants interoffice information delivered. Maybe your predecessor will give you an orientation as you begin your new job. Or maybe you should ask your boss directly. Either way, don't let too much time pass before you become savvy to the ways of the office.

That job you save may be your own.

19

How to Be the Political Player

So you say you're not a political animal. Even the thought of office politics makes you groan with dread. Well, get over it.

No one can escape politics. You have to deal politically with people all around you—in your home life, at the grocer's, and at your children's school. Everyone has interests that they're trying to move forward. You do too. You owe it to yourself to learn how to play the game.

Business is a game with rules and players of various levels of skills. Once you learn how to master the rules of office politics, you might actually find it fun. You'll see that what you're doing isn't the evil manipulation that you've been dreading. These are just *techniques* you apply every day to get the job done. Think of it as software that you'll be running. It's only as good or as evil as your purposes for it. You can use politics to make the workplace a happier, successful, and more smoothly running environment.

Feel better now?

Like software, the techniques of office politics have certainly evolved and developed over the years. You wouldn't dream of using a version of word processing software that was released thirteen years ago. It's difficult, it's indirect, and there is a lot of coding to memorize.

But state-of-the-art software is so advanced, you hardly even know you're running it. It's streamlined, effective, and efficient. It's user friendly. You don't have to memorize coding—all those buried signals you're hoping will go unnoticed.

It's "intuitive." Like pressing the right command keys or opening up the dialog boxes that make the most sense, your actions—and interactions—are governed by what feels right. You can also work with windows, transparent for all to see your motivations.

However, with software you're creating files. With the old model of office politics you would have been conquering your enemies and converting the undecided. The old model of office politics promotes bringing down the people around you to make yourself look better. That's a terrible way to go about doing business and cultivating your career. It creates unhappiness, not only in the vanquished but eventually within yourself.

Yesterday's power was built on fear. Today's power is built on charisma. Today, political superiority is based on respect, admiration, and loyalty. With New Millennium politics, you're creating *constituencies*. All these people need your help, and you're there to serve them. And in serving them, you get to stay in office.

The first step is to choose your constituency base wisely. Savvy players know that the first winning move is to find work in a company that promotes positive, mutually supportive relationships up and down the ranks. In that kind of healthy environment, you are free and encouraged to strengthen your power base by your willingness to strengthen the position of the others around you.

The objectives of today's office politics are the same as yesterday's: to gain the competitive advantage and to push through your own agendas. However, the competitive advantage you're advancing is the entire company's and the agendas are your department's. And, where once you would be considered the victor if you were the only one left standing after the smoke clears, today's politics value success to the benefit of *everyone*.

Here are some ways you can achieve the power you need without losing the loyalty and admiration you deserve:

ANTICIPATE THE NEEDS OF YOUR PEERS

A department that you're close to is suffering a crunch period. You find you have a spare half hour, or maybe you're even willing to give up your lunch hour. Don't wait to be asked for help. Walk right up, sit yourself down, and start licking those envelopes, grab that stack of folders to file . . . whatever it takes to help your counterpart make his or her deadline. (Don't forget to enter it into your task log.) This attitude reinforces the contemporary work ethic of teamwork and project management.

You're *project* oriented, not *job-description* oriented. With projects, the potential to learn and do new things is boundless. With job descriptions, it's as they say in the theater: "If it's not on the page, it's not on the stage." When people are considering you for promotions and raises, do you want them to be looking at that three-paragraph piece of paper? Or do they want to talk about "that time when you . . ." and "then there's that time when you . . ." "Oh, and look here, I almost forgot." Your task log reminds us that you also did this and this and this.

UNDER-REACT

There was a perfume advertisement on television a while back that said, "If you want to get someone's attention, whisper." Nothing will get you noticed faster than a totally unanticipated response to a crisis. If you want to really stand out as a front runner, keep your head. Especially when others would expect a major eruption from a lesser mortal. Sometimes I think that what I'm really being paid for is not to have a panic attack. The other services I provide are just the extras. Oh, you can blow your stack. That's one reaction choice. And you've probably seen a lot of managers do that, causing the staff to scurry around like mice. Afterward, they're depleted, and the fear of yet another eruption is a constant energy drain . . . leaving no electricity for the creative spark.

Or you can contain the crisis with an even-handed remark, such as "That's certainly doable" or "That's no big deal, we can fix that right up." Be the one to set the panic parameters and everyone will say, "Well, okay, I can go along with that." What they'll actually be doing is going along with *you*.

Along the same lines, calmly admit any mistakes you make. Even when they're costly or time consuming. But don't get caught up in some kind of abusive backwash. Contain your supervisor's reaction by containing yours. Sound horrified and morally repulsed by yourself, and your supervisor might think, "Well you are certainly taking your job seriously." But you're also assuming a submissive posture that every jungle animal knows is an invitation to rip you apart.

If you notice that your supervisor is building up a head of steam, don't get defensive. Calmly put up your hand and simply say, "I'll get right on it." Fix it, show you've fixed it, and help your supervisor move on to the next wonderful thing the two of you have to work on together.

Be the Teacher

Find one, two, or three individuals coming up right behind you. Make it your job to help them make their dreams come true. Maybe you don't have all the answers to their particular sets of goals, but you're one or two steps ahead of them. You can at least help them get to where you are.

These are not necessarily individuals you're grooming to succeed you. These are just good-potential workers that you've taken under your wing because it's the right thing to do. Remember, your objective here is to build your constituency. By resisting the temptation to have specific plans for them, they may one day show up years from now, ready to help you realize your next set of dreams.

Teachers learn by teaching others. When you sit down and decide exactly how you want to advise your protégés, you are actually calling into action your wisest self. And your wisest self will be advising you as well. You'll be amazed at how smart and office savvy you really are.

One last piece of advice here. Make sure your pupils have picked one, two, or three individuals for them to tutor in turn. Pass your power and wisdom on down the line. This way you're gardening the company, selecting the finest young sprouts, and growing them to best suit the company's overall mission. *And* you'll teach the next generation of teachers.

TAKE ON THE HIDEOUS JOB

Conventional wisdom tells us that the way to get ahead is to find the *one* task no one else wants to do and then do it. Don't feel that you must take on all the dirty work. After all, you don't want to be the company's beast of burden. But there's plenty that needs to be done that isn't being done by anyone with a specific job description. Best still, try to pick an expertise that has a lot of money associated with it: meeting planning, learning new software, learning how to train others in the new software, or learning how to install motherboards in the computers. Try to pick something that the company is spending a lot of money on in outsourced services. Learn how to do that, and then let your people know.

A minor detail: Try to make it a job you can at least tolerate. Once you learn how to do it, you'll be doing it a lot. Haven't you wondered how many times James Taylor has sung the song "Fire and Rain," and why he hasn't just spontaneously combusted right there on the stage for being so sick of that song? If you're going to learn how to do something, be sure you will be able to stomach it until you've had the chance to teach it to someone new. *Then teach someone new!*

GETTING NEXT TO THE BOSS

It used to be that to play up to the boss you had to leave yourself behind. You had to wear the same kinds of clothes he or she did. You had to join his country club and schedule your tee time for the same afternoons he did, even though you were missing out on your regular Parcheesi group. Well, here's a little insight: Your boss is probably out there hollering

"Fore!" because his boss is out there. And your boss is probably wondering where there might be a good Parcheesi game in town. All the while, *his* boss is really pining for a good game of canasta. But golf is where the contacts are made, so . . .

Isn't that just tragic?

If you hate playing this particular game (I mean the political one, not the golf), there's also an excellent chance that you would hate working for a boss who is impressed by that particular kind of political gambit. Still, there is no question that encounters with the boss away from the office are a great way to solidify your relationship with him or her. What you need is a shared experience, the two of you working side by side, with no hierarchy in place.

Volunteer to organize a departmental community service day (see Chapter 26, "Secretary's Day . . . Who Needs It?" for more ideas). If you want to impress the boss you already have, try to identify what kinds of causes or charity events he or she would be particularly excited about. A marathon? A fund-raising ball or banquet? A day refurbishing a house? A bike-a-thon? A day at a homeless shelter? Pull together three to five activity options that your boss can select from.

Then develop that project for your entire department so that there's a sense of completion at day's end. If you're going to work on a house for Habitat for Humanity, for instance, make sure the home is completely painted and the keys fit the locks in the new door by sundown. That satisfying feeling of finishing a job and putting away your tools is a very rare and sweet experience, especially in today's service industry. Be the one to give that to your boss and your colleagues. They'll remember you as the one who gets it done. Whatever it is.

Another thought about off-duty boss relationships: Off-duty encounter opportunities are an excellent way to meet potential employers. Lasting relationships of all sorts begin with chance encounters and shared interests. We all know that most advertisements for sweethearts placed in the personals columns are doomed to failure. Why should we expect a much better track record from responses to the help wanteds?

If you want a better chance of finding potential employers

with shared values, do what the lonely hearts advisors tell us to do: *Get out there!* Get involved with group activities that fire you up! Nice people volunteer. Energetic, visionary, optimistic people volunteer.

I only want to work with energetic, visionary, optimistic, nice people. Don't you?

BE CHOOSY ABOUT THE COMPANY YOU KEEP

I do not mean to say, "Be a social climber." That's an obvious ploy and quickly wins you disrespect and cultivates enemies. Treat the mailroom clerk with as much dignity as the assistant to the president. No matter who needs your attention, response, or service, they deserve it served up with courtesy, friendliness, and mutual respect.

But I do mean that you should stay away from energy vacuums, complainers, and oddballs. Gravitate toward positive people—especially if there's something going on in another area of your life that's bringing you down. Let their sunny outlook catch fire in your own heart. The complainers will just make you see work and life through mud-colored glasses. And whatever positive energy you might be bringing with you will just be siphoned away.

KEEP A FEW SECRETS TO YOURSELF

You are a box of laundry detergent. You've got the stuff to do the job, but, let's face it: Flakes are flakes. So you pretty up the actual container. You provide great colors, great design, and terrific marketing copy announcing for all the world to see exactly what you're capable of doing. That copy is your résumé, your reputation, the way you're known to the outside world. Your public knows what you can do, how much of your effort is necessary to get the job done, and how long it will take.

But is that box transparent so that your customers—your constituencies—can actually see the flakes? I don't think so.

Do they care about the molecular structures of the chemicals that go into making that flake? Again, I don't think so.

Those flakes are your trade secret. Your constituencies just want to know that you get the job done. Your opposition might be interested in how, but that's your trade secret. Let them marvel. Let them wonder.

Because you're marvelous. And you're wonderful. What a dynamic platform on which to build your own political campaign!

—————— PROFILE ——————

Tammie Ball
Secretary
Computer Science Corporation
Wall, NJ

Until I got this job, I had no idea what it was like to be really happy at work.

I was once the only administrative secretary in an office of forty-five people. But my main responsibility was to assist the director, who ran the office by playing on people's fear. It was terrible.

She was the type of boss who had favorites. Those who were her favorites, she totally protected. Those who weren't, she didn't even speak to. I was her secretary and for the last four or five months she didn't even speak to me. She would walk by my desk without even saying hello.

There were many times she would run through the office screaming, "I'm going to fire everybody!" One minute she would be fine, then something would trigger her and then she would start screaming at you. Many times she would call me into her office and scream at me because of something someone else did. Then she would calm down, say, "Thank you I needed to vent," and dismiss me from her office . . . like our meeting was over. I felt like I must have been carrying a sign that read, "Scream at me."

There were many people who would go to the human resources department and complain about her. HR's reaction would be to pick up the phone, say to her, "You have a problem with such and such a person, please handle it."

In the beginning (when she was talking to me), she would tell me how she hated men, in particular her husband. But she would always protect herself, so she didn't look sexist. When she hired a new team, she would always throw one man in there just to protect herself.

And she would try to make me think I was nuts. She'd come in in the morning and say, "The proposal that I left on your desk last night, have you made the changes yet?" After fifteen minutes of blaming me for losing it, she would find it in her office, and simply say, "Oh, here it is, I forgot to give it to you."

Eventually I caught on. But in the beginning I use to think, "Oh my God, what did I do with that proposal?" I would search my work area in a total panic.

I don't usually take this kind of guff. But when it was my boss, I was afraid to say anything because I could get myself fired. I would question myself and my own sanity. I'd think, "I must be overreacting to what's going on, it really can't be this bad. Maybe I'm inviting it somehow."

Everything changed one summer when the daughter of a vice president from one of the sister companies came to work as a summer intern. She was able to confirm to me that, no, it wasn't all in my head. She'd say all the time, "I can't believe what these people do to you."

But I was beaten down so much that I couldn't see myself going through the process of finding a new job. I talked myself back into being positive. It was difficult for me to start pulling myself back up. But I did it a little at a time, going back over old reference letters and positive reviews from other employers. The act of starting the process of looking for a new job made me happier and stronger at work. My boss didn't bother me quite so much, because I knew something she didn't: I was on my way out of there.

Now I work for Computer Science Corporation. Wow, what a culture shock! There is really a whole other world out there beyond the misery I was enduring every day.

I wake up in the morning and I want to go to work. Everyone is so nice. I walk into my new company and there's no tension in the air. My boss is usually in already, and greets me with a "Good morning, how was your evening?" I'm not there for friendship, but it's just nice to know there's a normal human being who takes an interest in who I am as a human being, not just as a slave.

I vow I'm never going to let another human being ever do what my former boss did to me again.

1. *Leave.* If people treat you horribly at work, get out of that job! Don't even second-guess yourself.

2. *Don't let anyone knock out your self-esteem.* If you know what you're worth, stick with that and don't let anyone tell you otherwise.

3. *Try to remember that there is a different world.* Yes, even though it seems totally hopeless and that there is nothing else out there for you. The quicker you get out, the easier it will be to package yourself as a confident, capable, valuable candidate.

4. *Don't isolate yourself.* Keep your contacts fresh and current. While you're unhappy, they'll be there to tell you that you deserve better. And when you're ready to take matters in your own hands and start looking for a new job, they'll be there with all sorts of referrals and job leads.

20

LEADERSHIP IN
CORPORATE AMERICA
. . . YES! YOU!

This is just my humble opinion, but all across the country
bookstore clerks are shelving the books wrong.

Walk into any bookstore and you'll see what I mean. All
the business management books are lumped together. This is
where we find the autobiographies by the corporate greats,
everyone from the chairman of Chrysler to the president of
Starbucks. Without question, these are really inspiring models
of leadership, vision, nerve, and entrepreneurship. This is the
section where captains of industry go to read more about
themselves, and to think about ways to lead their employees
out of whatever muck and mire their company happens to be
in at the moment. All very useful stuff. And one of their recur-
ring themes is how to motivate that great mass of people
called *employees*.

People who read these books are trying to absorb quick
wisdom pills on how to become a leader. And then they can
motivate the likes of you. What bothers me about many of
these books is that they seem to assume employees (like you)
are as dumb as dial tones.

And where are *you* in the bookstore? If you usually don't
consider yourself management material, I bet I'll find you way
over there on a totally different aisle and bookshelf—the one
with books on career management, parachutes, finding the
job hat that fits . . . all those marvelous books that tell you how

to design the career that means the most to you and your life goals.

Well, you're motivated all right. You're in the bookstore reading about out how to find a leadership style that best matches your motivations.

What if we found a way to somehow bring all those books together in one section? Remember that Reese's candy commercial in which the two characters bump into each other? "Hey, you got peanut butter on my chocolate." "Well, you got chocolate in my peanut butter!" Mmmmm. Revelation! A new product!

So, okay, we do that with the books, using them to bring so-called leadership together with the so-called rank and file. You'd find yourself standing right next to your prominent neighborhood CEO, perhaps both of you peering over your shoulders to get a peek at what the other one is reading.

There are two things I'd like to see happen: Mr. or Ms. Big suddenly gets a revelation and thinks, "Say, my employees are already motivated. I just have to become the leader they deserve to have."

And I'd like to see you discover for yourself, "Say this leadership business isn't the brain surgery I thought it was! I could do that!"

Oh the things you could teach the management level!

I'd like you to market yourself—even if it's only to yourself—as a leader. You don't have to be CEO to lead your constituencies to greatness. You don't have to ask permission to be a leader. In fact, that's where a lot of management material fail to achieve leadership: They're waiting for permission. Leaders don't need permission.

Whoever says "You may" to a real leader? Even real leaders themselves don't say "You may." They say "You can! You will! You want to!" Because real leaders lead from the heart. And they lead the hearts of their constituencies.

There's not a job description, employment contract, or résumé in the world that says "Lead from the heart." So it follows that the people who do it . . . just do it.

So why not you? The executive desk is no more a permission or empowerer of leadership to the manager than the assistant's desk is a *barrier* to leadership.

You have the power to assume leadership! This doesn't mean you have to weasel your way into the boardroom. It doesn't mean you have to affect your company's performance on Wall Street. It doesn't mean you have to stage a coup against the current formal power team. Or step on the heads of other assistants in a claw to the top.

I'm talking about the New Leadership that takes a vision for what the future promises and leads your team willingly and joyfully to it. And you can start small, even if it's only to organize a monthly brown-bag interdepartmental luncheon at first.

Leadership is a power that's within your reach. You just have to be willing to stand up, step forward, and say, "I'm ready."

Ready?

A Crisis in Leadership

Not to wish ill on your employer, but a crisis in leadership is your best opportunity to step forward and take some measure of control. The chances are excellent that there's some kind of crisis of leadership in your company right now. No organization is perfect; it's made up of human beings, complete with all their flaws. What do you expect?

It's important to keep in mind that crises don't even have to be negative. The dictionary defines "crisis" as a turning point at which the outcome can be either better or worse. But it's at this turning point that the company is the most unstable, and this could be your chance to seize a leadership role and save the day.

Crises come in many forms, some of which no organization can prevent. As I'm finishing up the manuscript for this book, the sad news came across the wires that Roberto Goitzueta, the longtime, respected chairman of Coca-Cola, passed away from lung cancer. He was diagnosed not even two months ago. Now he's gone.

How many crises do you suppose that great company is facing right now? The man was important on the world stage of business, so I'm sure all sorts of systems are in place for his successor. But the ripple effects of such a sudden passing will probably still be evident well into the next century. Careers of those closest to him might be derailed. His hand-picked staff might be displaced by the assistants loyal to the executive who assumes his chair.

From the mail room to the lunchroom to the boardroom, and throughout the world, there will be new discussions about the direction of Coca-Cola. The company's leaders must achieve a new shared vision of the company's future, and then bring along its many thousands of employees, customers, and vendors, each one coping in his or her own way with the shock and grief of the chairman's passing.

A crisis of this scope happens rarely in any company. But daily there is opportunity to assume leadership on every level. Overall, the negative result of a leadership crisis happens when there is fear and distraction. This can happen, and does daily, in many different ways:

• With companies still flattening their staffing levels, upper-level through middle-management employees are especially susceptible to the distractions of their own career concerns. As a result they're not thinking quite so clearly. They're letting details fall through the cracks. They're neglecting important relationships. This is your opportunity to step forward to pick up what they've dropped.

• A power struggle at the top may be pulling the company apart, dividing loyalties and creating intrigue. Such stories are epic, and they'll probably continue until companies and other power structures are completely taken over by computers. The fractured organization will be confused, its staff running in every direction; lots of energy will be expended, very little will result. Yours might be the only steady hand. Grab that wheel, whatever it takes. Your leadership may be the only thing standing between the company's future and Chapter 11.

• A manager may be going through a personal crisis, such as a divorce, financial problems, substance abuse, or the death of a parent. Whether the trouble is short-term or long-term, you are probably in the best position to pinch-hit on his or her behalf. Run that scheduled sales meeting, keep whatever appointments you can to at least keep your department updated on breaking news in your industry, make the calls he or she would have made, or volunteer to draft reports that only need a quick edit and final signature.

As you assume more responsibility upward, give yourself a break by sending more of your routine duties downward to the next tier of assistants. They should jump at the chance to take on new tasks and prove themselves worthy of your level.

• The company is reacting to shareholder demands by instituting drastic cost-cutting measures. Or a merger on the horizon means the possible layoff of a huge percentage of your colleagues. Consider putting together an outplacement package for your colleagues. Talk with the human resources manager and suggest that the company budget for outplacement counseling and skills training for your peers. Unfortunately, your level is frequently overlooked when companies are planning personal/executive development programs. Step forward and speak up. You'll gain admiration and loyalty. Just because these people may be gone from your company doesn't mean the effort won't be returned to you later in the form of a fantastic network and grapevine.

• A consumer or employee lawsuit is siphoning management's attention away from its mission and toward damage control. Sales must still be made. Customers must still be serviced. New prospects must still be cultivated. Payroll must still be met.

It's hard to focus on a lofty mission when your head is spinning. This is true.

But it is also true that you can stop the dizziness by focusing on a distant point. Be the one to let that distant point be a better future, and you can be one of the points of calm that lead the company back to stability.

Stabilize yourself by envisioning and working toward an objective that is consistent with the company's overall mission, even if it's a seemingly minor one, such as saving money on office supplies. Eventually you'll influence your manager, who will eventually influence his or her supervisor, who will eventually influence up the ranks. It may sound simplistic, and yes, this is ideal-world thinking. But somebody's got to establish a serene foundation from which to build the future. Why not you?

THE STUFF OF LEADERSHIP . . . IF NOT YOU, WHO?

Leadership tasks are within your area of influence. The company has just published a new mission statement. How can you take the lead in putting it into action? Your department has just initiated a recycling program. How can you take the lead in encouraging staffers to put their used paper into the yellow bin instead of the trash can?

In his book *On Leadership*, John W. Gardner outlines the fundamental tasks of leadership. You may be in the habit of thinking that leadership happens in the executive suite, but when you see this list, you'll agree that leadership happens at your desk as well.

• *Envisioning goals.* Identify how your short-term goals serve the long-term mission of your company. Play them out in your imagination. Your value to the firm will then be obvious. And you'll be able to more effectively market yourself to your supervisors and recruit others to work in keeping with your own objectives.

• *Affirming values.* In many cases, you are the employer's

front gate to the public—its front gate to its constituency. You can be your company's values in action. Affirm the company's values by your professionalism, kindness, and attitude of service.

• *Motivating.* No matter where you are on the organization chart, you can motivate your colleagues up and down the ranks. Your attitude, behavior, and ability to express your vision will inspire those closest to you to achieve even more.

• *Managing.* You may not have the title of manager, but you certainly do your share of managing. You manage time, you set priorities, you manage your supervisor's schedule, you even get to decide who has access and who doesn't.

• *Achieving workable unity.* A company must be diverse. Each department has a different function. The way you interact with your fellow assistants, the way you share information and news, the way you help and ask for help in return—these are all the building bridges to relationships, rapport, and shared visions of a common goal.

• *Explaining.* Katharine Hepburn advises, "Never complain, never explain." That's all very well and good for Kate, but few of us can pull that off. Nor should we. Explaining leads to understanding; understanding leads to relationships. Relationships boost a company's prospects far beyond its originally envisioned mission.

• *Serving as a symbol.* You can have as high a profile as you want. Determine what you want your own actions to represent: Patience? Organization? Courtesy? Courage? And symbolize those virtues by your behavior.

• *Representing the group.* You represent the company, you represent your supervisor, and you represent your peers. You represent your group to itself. Do its members like what they see about themselves when they watch you in action?

• *Renewal.* This is Gardner's last distinction of what makes a leader. By taking fresh approaches to your work—by reading this book, for instance, and sharing what you learned—you can't help but renew your department. You are not the same person you were before you picked up this book. By bringing a newer, more educated self to work, you help those working around you to renew their own methods of working.

As you read these tasks of leadership, I'll bet you were thinking, "Wow, I'm already doing that, and this, and this, and that." Well, knowing the kind of work you do, I'm not at all surprised. Your leadership skills are probably extremely well exercised. You just didn't realize that you could attach such a lofty label to those everyday things you do.

As you go through your day. And as you start considering all those entries in your task log, think about how much leadership is attached to each one. And when the time comes for your performance appraisal, make sure those tasks and accomplishments are recognized.

You're leadership material. Do your supervisors a favor by letting them know. That's what a leader would do.

21

How to Stuff a Wild Work Day

In the old days, one of the principle jobs of assistants was to save their supervisor's time. That's why they answered the phone. That's why they did the typing. That's why they ran interference at the door, to keep the riffraff from barging in.

Unfortunately, that particular aspect of your job description was never refined out of existence. Never mind the fact that your workload resembles that of a middle manager, it's still your job to be interrupted. This makes it very difficult to see projects through from beginning to end. It's impossible to carry on a business conversation of any depth or complexity. How, for instance, can you negotiate the best room rate for the conference coming up when your credibility is chiseled away every time you must say to the salesperson, "I'm sorry we keep getting interrupted, would you mind holding one more time?"

I wish I could responsibly advise you to shout, "Hey! Wait in line, why don't you?" every time someone scurries up to you with an urgent, super-urgent, or ASAP project. I know that's what I have wanted to do. Even today, as an independent businessperson, the words sometimes come very dangerously close to my lips. But I smile, say something positive, and figure out where it fits into my priorities when I have the chance to think about it more.

But, unfortunately, you don't have the luxury of prioritizing your own work. You take it as it comes. And sometimes it comes fast and furious. And, maybe you have the chance to think to yourself, "I'd take a time management class if I had the time."

Even though it's your job to be of service to your department, it's very costly to you to be *constantly* at the end of the yoyo string of other people's priorities. Come and go, back and forth, wait in line, give up your place in line to someone who's busier, start a sentence, get interrupted. Sit down, stand up. Sit down again. Poise your fingers on the computer keyboard only to then reach for the ringing telephone.

This is a costly lifestyle because it gives you absolutely no time to consider, to balance, or to prioritize. What do you suppose your supervisor is doing behind that quiet door? Considering, balancing, and prioritizing.

T.S. Eliot, the poet who wrote the poem on which the musical *Cats* is based, also wrote a beautiful, epic poem called *The Love Song of J. Alfred Prufrock*. In it he wrote, "I have measured out my life with coffee spoons."

It's easy to do that when you're too frantic to sit back and just consider. Bit by bit, your life pours away into someone else's coffee cup. I know you don't want that. At least not forever. But how can you keep it from being forever when you're too busy dribbling your life away in tiny amounts: just the amount of time, for instance, that it takes to wait in line at the photocopy machine.

So you may not have a chance to take a time management class. You're too busy taking up the slack while your supervisor's in that class. Well let's just take a couple of minutes right now and go over some principles on stuffing a wild work day, and leaving yourself some time to breathe and dream.

MORE PRODUCTIVITY, LESS TIME

ESTABLISH A NO-FLY ZONE

In Washington, D.C., there is a space of air over the White House and the Capitol in which no planes are allowed to fly. Ever. Except for maybe the official presidential helicopter.

That's a no-fly zone. You can have one, too. Establish a time in your day when no one, absolutely no one, is allowed to interrupt you (unless it's your family on the way to the hospital). This is the time set aside to do uninterruptible work. I'd like to suggest relatively mindless work, like filing. While one part of your brain is focusing on the alphabetical or numerical orders, let the rest of your mind swing free and easy. Let the ideas, tensions, and fantasies drift up to the surface and float away. Eventually a stroke of brilliance or an insight will reveal itself. A problem will be solved, a fortune-making idea will appear, or you'll just be relaxed by the time you re-enter the day's usual pace.

This hour is crucial time. And it's extremely productive. This is when genius strikes. Creativity consultants will tell you that if you want the solution to a bothersome puzzle, think about other things. It works for me. One year I was wrestling with one of my first computer setups, but I couldn't get it to work. Now this was an expensive system, costing about three times as much as a computer system today. Of course, it only did a fraction of what my pocket calculator can do now. But the fact that I had spent all this money and it wasn't coming together as quickly as I had hoped was really beginning to bug me. So I turned my attention to proofreading an article I had just written. Not twenty minutes into the proofreading task, the computer solution came to me. It was as though someone was showing me a slide show of exactly what to do, how to hook everything up, and how to turn it on.

How do you establish that no-fly zone? Use your leadership skills, of course. You're not the only one who craves an hour a day of calm, interruption-free work. If you are part of the team that shares lunch-hour receptionist duty, you already know the principle. Pool your resources with the other assistants. Work out some kind of round-robin schedule so that everyone has at least one hour of breathing space daily. That's over and above the regular lunch hour.

I'm way ahead of you . . . you're probably thinking, "My boss would never go for that." Probably not. Not until you repackage your services to the company. On paper they're paying you by the hour, and each hour you're expected to follow instructions. But in reality (and it's important to me that you get this), you are really marketing the skills and services you provide during a set number of hours. Like your supervisor, your job is to attain goals and objectives. Your job is not to turn yourself into the Energizer Bunny hour after hour.

Get support from the top by pointing out to your supervisor that the last great stroke of genius (obviously you don't want to say *genius* but you get what I mean) you had was during a quiet time away from the hectic pace of interruptions. Tell her that you just read this dynamite book on time management and that the author pointed out that assistants could really add much more to the company's goals if they were given just an hour every day (or every other day) to work and think without the constant potential for interruption.

Tell her that you'd like to at least give it a try. And that you've coordinated with the other assistants and that she will never even notice a compromise in the service she's accustomed to. She'll get the calls she wants, she won't get the calls she doesn't want. Reassure her that this program will be managed by the assistants themselves with no management intervention necessary. Ever.

Support from the highest possible level will go far in ensuring your success with this experiment. You'll get the respect from management for initiating such a plan. And you will get the gratitude from your colleagues who crave that quiet hour as much as you do.

Other common time management techniques are:

1. *Do only one thing at a time.* Surprised? Of course. You're used to behaving like one of those cartoon octopuses, each tentacle holding a phone receiver, steno pad, or pen. But have you noticed how energy-draining it is to feel guilty about all the things you're not doing while you're concentrating on something else? Cut yourself a break, and at least once or twice a day resist the urge to load up that extra tentacle. So you're on hold for a few minutes, you really don't have to

write out those invitation envelopes that very minute. Do it the next time you're on hold.

2. *Urge your supervisors to take up E-mail.* This is a considerable time savings for you. Every E-mail they fire off is one less memo or letter that you have to format and type out. But that's not how you persuade your supervisors. What you tell your supervisors is that E-mails get much faster notice and response than conventional hard-copy correspondence. "Snail mail," the old-fashioned letters that come via the post office, usually arrive several days later. E-mail is instantly delivered—a result that might cost as much as $15 with an overnight delivery or telegram service. E-mail gives your supervisors clout, credibility, and timely response.

3. *Encourage your supervisors to place their own phone calls.* Yes, placing calls through you can be a time-saver for your supervisors, but this practice is considered pretentious and annoying to the recipients of the phone call. By the time your supervisors get around to picking up the phone, the party waiting on the other end is extremely annoyed. I have one friend who routinely says no when she hears an assistant ask, "Will you hold for Mr. Whozits?"

Likewise, unless it's the briefest of messages—such as confirming a lunch appointment—*strongly urge your supervisors to leave their own voice-mail messages* instead of asking you to do it. Hierarchies still exist, even in the most egalitarian organizations. And most professionals don't take kindly to being instructed by their colleagues' assistants. This saves time all around. You're out of the loop, so you can concentrate on a more valuable project. And the message is uttered only once: from the supervisor's lips into the voice-mail service of the recipient.

4. *Coordinate your flex-time.* If your company offers flex-time, and if you're free to have hours that differ from your supervisors', try to get either a later morning and or later evening. This way you can work in peace, finishing up the day's workload after they have left. The second best option is to come in a couple of hours earlier, but it is extremely difficult

to leave earlier when there's a busy day in full swing. And you'll find you're just working longer and longer hours. Try to avoid keeping the same hours they do. You are never ever quite caught up, and will always be in some kind of reactive mode.

Whatever time-saving mechanisms you install, the main point is to seize control of at least part of your workday. This will be the time you can strategize, scheme, and dream, while still being professional and productive. These could be the hours during which you build your future.

As Eliot wrote in *The Love Song of J. Alfred Prufrock,* "And indeed there will be time to wonder, 'Do I dare?' and 'Do I dare?' "

Go on ahead and dare. You have plenty of time.

22

"Yes Stress" and How to Avoid It

Saying yes can kill you. Did you know that? When you must always say yes regardless of your true feelings, it shows that you have little control over your work life. Researchers in Britain released a study in 1997 that confirmed that having little control at work can cause heart disease. A study of English civil servants showed that it wasn't the top executives who die of heart attacks but the administrative staff.

I call that "yes stress."

But you don't want its polar opposite, either: "No? Then go!"

Now before we move any further into this chapter, I want to get one thing straight. I'm not advising you to be stubborn or unproductive or insubordinate. I'm assuming that you're already a top-notch team player, eager to cooperate, willing to compromise, and always first in line for a new project.

Right? Right. Then let's continue.

It's unfortunate, but it's a fact: Undesirable work flows downhill. And even in the most evolved of teams, the administrative/support function is downhill. It's a simple law of gravity that all the stuff no one else wants to do will accumulate at your desk. That includes paperwork, errands, handling unpleasant phone calls, and even delivering bad news.

Read this carefully and remember it: Whatever you are not willing to say no to, you *will* be expected to say yes to.

So the boundaries begin with you. I think every member of the support staff should say no once in a while. There should be a good reason, of course, but just as every parent or friend should exercise the right to say no, you need to demonstrate to those around you that you do have your limits.

And if you don't? Here's what can happen:

- You become overworked. You end up staying later, coming in earlier, skipping meals, making more mistakes, and wrecking your reputation.
- You lose sight of departmental priorities.
- You're too busy to remember your own career priorities.
- You don't delegate appropriate tasks to others.
- You get so caught up in "people pleasing," you don't have time to realize that you're pleasing no one and that you have lost the respect of the group.

Every time you say yes to something, you say no to everything else in the entire universe that could have taken its place. Say yes to the first job that comes along, and you might pull yourself out of the running for your dream job. Say yes, yes, yes to every assignment that's flopped on your desk (with no regard to the task log, I might add) and you've lost the efficiency that you are being paid to provide.

In short, say yes to everything and you're robbing both the company and yourself of a high-quality performance.

But say no the wrong way and you will also lose faith and credibility as a team player.

Here's the secret: Make your team accountable for the ways it asks you to help meet its goals. *Performance*—that's what it's all about. The company doesn't care who loves you or who has a grudge. The company wants measurable results from your team. And that's the main thing you have in common with your supervisors. That's the common goal.

Here's the one word you should never use when saying no: "No." "No" is a spit in the face. "No" is a wall. "No" is the end of all negotiation. "No" will be the end of your job.

How about other rationales instead?

"I'd love to process that budget of yours right now, Last-

Minute Bob, but if I drop Money-Making Mary's proposal, we will miss the deadline and lose the chance to bid. I'll get right on it tomorrow."

This demonstrates your willingness—no, your *eager-ness*—to cooperate. But, like everyone else on the team, your eye is on the profit ball. And reason makes it clear that you must meet that proposal deadline instead.

Or rely on the task log.

"Sure, Bob. Why don't you check the log and see who might be willing to give you their priority position. Let me know what the two of you decide."

Your team members are as responsible to you as you are to them. Setting up the work task log is your way of giving everyone equal access to the big picture of your workday. In many ways, you are like one of those cow diagrams at the butcher's—all divvied up in parts. Let them fight over who gets what part.

It will also put them in the habit of frequently referring to the task log. Eventually, one of them will have to ask, "Hey, what does all this blue and green ink mean?" And then you get to tell them. Up goes your stock.

Or pass the buck.

"Sure, Bob. You know, I handled the budget within a week of coming to work here. That was a great learning oppor-tunity. Jim's been here awhile. I'll bet he's up for the challenge now. I'll train him when I have some time. Or, if you're in a hurry, maybe you can show him the ropes."

You're still on Bob's side. Together you're solving his problem. And you're demonstrating that you have an organi-zational mind, already knowing exactly who would be the best choice for the job—and brilliantly positioning the pass as doing Jim a favor. What genius! Pull out that yellow pen! There goes another career blocker!

Return the serve.

"Oh Bob! It's about that time for budget, isn't it? I thought you'd be coming my way soon. So look what I've done for you. I've automated the process for you on this disk.

Just plug in the numbers as you develop them and you're done!"

Demonstrate anticipatory management. Anticipate the assignment and figure out how to get the job back on your team member's desk. Oh, I know what you're thinking: "But Bob wants the budget off his desk to begin with."

That's probably true. But then you must ask yourself: "Am I a partner on this team or its servant?" If you're its servant, go right ahead and pile up all those assignments. But if you're a partner whose role it is to be *of service*, then it's your job to anticipate and streamline processes. If Bob's going through the budget format anyway, you will remove several steps of the process by making it easier for him to plug in the numbers as he develops them. Then all he has to do is hit Control P and the document's on its way to the printer!

Managing up is easier than you thought, isn't it? (Please say yes!)

23

THE NEW GOLDEN RULE

Do you remember Nancy Johnson, one of our Voices of Success? She's the one who went from a hard-driving, brash, maybe even intimidating boss to working with a gentle, philosophical, sensitive soul who was equally successful, if not more so. Can you imagine the culture shock she went through when she received her first time-sensitive assignment from this new supervisor? Instead of creating the 911 situation that she was accustomed to, he quietly approached her desk and said, "I'd like you to do this for me."

Accustomed to fire alarms and sirens, Nancy figured this was just another project that could be done when she got around to it. Well, not so. Within a few hours Cliff was back at her desk, asking in a friendly, low-pressure way: "Is it done yet?"

Nancy was lucky. She got it quick. She instantly recognized that this was Cliff's 911 demeanor (well maybe not *quite* 911, maybe more like 711, but the clock was still ticking).

A quick, friendly conversation helped frame the episode in a way that showed them both how the other one communicated.

"So you want me to yell at you?" he asked.

"No, no, no," she laughed, happily wishing for just a little time to get used to this kinder approach to getting the same job done in the same amount of time.

They were lucky. It ended well. But how many other people find they just can't work with each other, primarily because of a little communication disconnect? How frustrating it is to continue to hammer away at the same attempt to communicate with someone but get no results. Over and over again.

We all have bad days, right? Well, one day I was unloading on a friend about a business relationship problem that never seemed to improve no matter how much I tried to get it straight. She simply said to me, "George-Anne, if you don't change your approach on this, the result is always going to be the same."

Bong. This simple principle kept ringing in my head: "If you always do it one way, you'll always get the same results. Change your method and you change your outcome."

Okay. Now I'm equipped to start making a change. But where do I begin? By putting a business twist on the Golden Rule, which is Do Unto Others as You Would Have Them Do Unto You.

Can't go wrong with that? Most times probably not. But in business, everyone you deal with is both a customer and a partner in some capacity. So you must update the rule with a customer service approach: Treat Others as They Would Want to Be Treated.

And this means adjusting your communication styles to both serve and motivate your business partners. But before you adjust your communication style, you must learn to recognize theirs. This little rule works in marriage, too, by the way.

Eight years ago I said to my husband, "Alan, come on, let's get out of D.C. Let's move to Annapolis. Cute little town. Lots of antiques. Lots of water for the boat of your dreams."

His response: "Okay, let's first study the infrastructure. Let's look at the political climate. Let's look at the school system. Let's sit outside in the car on a Friday night and count the number of parking spaces outside the restaurants."

Three months later: "Alan, let's move to Annapolis. Cute little town. Lots of antiques. Lots of water for the boat of your dreams. We'd really like living there."

His response: "One does not make a move like this overnight. One should study, survey, evaluate, and research. Then one should go back and quantify the study, the survey, the evaluation, and the research."

Three months later: "Alan, I'm moving."

Sometimes you have to learn the hard way. And I learned

that threat management does not work. You have to come up with more threats, and have them escalate in intensity. Then you have to act on them to get attention and keep respect. That's no way to run a marriage or a business.

If you want to powerfully sell your idea, you better have a different technique up your sleeve. This may be new to you, but it's easy. It involves only four major elements—the four major operating types. I'm not saying that you should bend your own behavior to suit the personality types that you report to. But I am submitting it for your consideration. You have to work with others, you have to live with your family. You need others to help you achieve your own goals. Is it a sign of weakness to give in to the ways others want to be treated? I don't think so. You are operating from a position of knowledge. And we all know that knowledge is . . . what? Power.

Here are the four personality types.

POWERBOATS

They want brief communication. No lengthy blah blah and background. Cut to the chase when presenting them with your ideas and proposals. Don't talk them to death. Don't paper them to death. They don't even need you to go through the customary social preliminaries, such as "Hi, how was your weekend?" You don't have to set things up, you don't have to set the stage, you don't even have to light the candles if you're dating one of them. Their bottom line is the bottom line: Results, not how you arrived at them.

These people are always up and positive. Winning is the only conceivable outcome for them. They are about solutions, not problems. Anything negative is a foreign planet to them. They think entrepreneurially, and they challenge the status quo every day. They love to shake things up, come up with new products, new ideas, new services, and new ways to make money. "Whatever it takes" is their motto.

"Just handle it" is how they give their marching orders. This is a great opportunity to demonstrate your own innovative nature. But if you're not a powerboat yourself, you might find your head spinning. But careful about what you say to them. They don't do negative, remember? So complainers, harpers, carpers, and fence-sitters don't stand a chance around them.

You'd think they would be the ideal employer, so efficient and everything. Well, they have one fatal flaw: They're terrible listeners. They are always preoccupied with the next thing, always driving forward to where they're going next, what they're doing next, or who they're seeing next. They're only half listening at any one time—if you're lucky. I know one woman who is always cranking away at new ideas. Sometimes her husband speaks to her for twenty minutes about something very important. Eventually, her eyes focus, and she looks at her husband as if she has had no idea he was there. And she says, "Oh sorry. I was in my 30 percent mode." Thankfully, for their marriage, they've both learned to laugh, and "30 percent mode" has become their shorthand for "Don't take it personally, I was just gone for a minute."

If you are supporting a powerboat supervisor, this is your chance to shine. Be a good listener when he isn't. Once he recognizes that you pick up details he misses, you're going to find yourself included in meetings. Once you've demonstrated that it's smart to take the time to double-check his work, you'll be given a little more time to accomplish that "get it done yesterday" task. Keep in touch with his hard-driving pace, and he'll take you with him all the way to the top.

JET SKIS

Jet ski people aren't needy, but they sure do look like it sometimes. They need interaction. They want to know how your weekend was. So when you play the game of withholding or are abrupt with them, you will end up spending twice as much time with them than you would have needed to. Slather them with information. Let them talk. Let them talk a lot. They are very verbal and very articulate (no wonder, they give themselves lots of practice).

They're also motivational and enthusiastic. You'll find yourself caught up in their spell. They love groups, committees, and parties. You'll find their sense of humor very entertaining. They care about you, they care about your happiness on the job, and they'll want to talk about how wonderful it is to have a convivial, upbeat, and nonconflicting work environment.

Sailboats

Sailboats are process-oriented, and since their motto is "Get it done thoroughly and get it right the first time," they have tremendous faith in their own accuracy. And they expect you to believe in them as well.

Their classic response to any question regarding the validity of their work is "Well, of course it's valid, I did it." Consequently they tend to come off a little condescending. Maybe even a lot condescending. But they don't mean to be offensive, any more than powerboats mean to be abrupt.

Because of their perfectionist approach to work (ever wonder who fills in the crossword puzzle with ink?), they also put a tremendous amount of pressure on themselves. They're self-critical, but it comes off as critical as others. They judge and evaluate everything. They know who comes in early, who stays late. And they hold grudges.

They like data—the who, what, when, where, why, and how of their world. And they like structure.

These are the people who strike fear and intimidation in the hearts of lesser souls. But you have their number, and you know that the heavy weather they might create around them is nothing compared to the way they must feel inside.

Sure, there are plenty of sailboats who delight in the processes of their lives, who relish the charts and the figures. And who are beloved and respected by all those around them. But if you pull the short straw, and find yourself teamed up with an unhappy sailboat, you have the advantage. Just whisper to yourself, "poor baby," and treat that person with a kind and unintimidated demeanor. You'll end up with a pussycat who actually volunteers to help you with your taxes.

Sailboats are very useful to have around the house, but you have to treat them right and endure a little too much detail—especially if you're a powerboat like me. Remember how I said my husband wanted to survey, measure, and count his way to Annapolis? We finally got our house on the water, but my lessons were only just beginning.

We came home after work one day, and Alan said, "Ah, the air-conditioning guys were here today."

"Great," I said, more focused on whether there was something microwaveable in the kitchen.

"Let me show you how to use this computerized system," he said. But I wanted to do dinner—well, actually I really wanted to just stay away from anything that called itself a computer. Alan was asking me to take a stroll through my fear zone. Hmmm, microwave? Nah, something that cooks long and slow and needs lots of close attention. That was the ticket for tonight's dinner.

"I'll get to the air-conditioning later," I said to Alan. And an argument ensued. He pushed, I pushed back. And one of the rare evenings we were home together was ruined.

All I had to do was indulge my beloved. Let him show me the air-conditioning, while I reserved my brain for mentally poking through the pantry. Then after dinner, I could have said, "Would you please show me again so I'll remember?"

Bingo! He gets his way (twice), I get my way. And dinner is a success. And the air-conditioning unit? I don't know. That's still his domain. It's got numbers and dials, and Alan just loves that.

And it works. The powerboat in me just loves *that*.

HOUSEBOATS

Houseboats are very accommodating and hospitable. This is how a houseboat sounds: "Sure, no problem. I'll do it. Sure.

Sure. Sure. You all go ahead, I'll get this done. Don't think twice about it."

Houseboats are the office songbirds. They have a high work ethic, and they're work magnets. But as much as that's their glory, it's also their downfall. They take on and take on until they get overwhelmed and then get sick. Their personalities may be houseboats, but their bodies draw the line. And force these chipper little creatures to bed. Watch out though, because they'll take work to bed with them.

Working with a houseboat supervisor is also a double-edged sword. You have a sunny temperament to look forward to working with every day. And you really won't have all that much work to do. Since they're so busy saying "sure," they forget to say "Hey, will you please?" As a result, they're delegation impaired. And you become learning impaired. You don't get the chance to grow and learn.

Houseboats are hard workers, and they will teach you a lot about being team members. But they won't teach you about leadership or about innovation. Oh, they have great ideas, but they don't know how to sell them to the decision makers.

Work with a houseboat, but make sure *you* bring to the team that spark and flash that promotes your team's innovations. This is a great opportunity for you to stand out as a key contributor. But when you make that acceptance speech at the next awards dinner, remember to point into the audience and say, "Ms. Houseboat, please stand up and take a bow." She'll say—what else—"Sure!"

Some people might think that I'm advising you to *manipulate* these different types by recognizing their buttons and pushing them to suit your purpose.

Sure, there's button-pushing involved here. No doubt. But I'd like to exchange the word *manipulate* for the word *accommodate*. Weak, powerless people manipulate because that's the only way they think they can achieve their goals.

Accommodation comes from a place of power. Be strong and confident in your own abilities to affect a change. And give ground to your teammates, your partners, to function in the way they're happiest.

It's like the definition of etiquette. You're behaving in a way that makes everyone comfortable. As far as I'm concerned, that's the most straightforward and powerful position to be in. Don't you agree?

——— 24 ———

THE BEST WAY TO INVEST
A QUARTER

Are you like me? Did you grow up watching your parents read the newspaper and then nod knowledgeably about all those strange names in all those strange places? How *did* they know what was going on? How *did* they know who was who? How *did* they know when something was true or "just another pack of lies"? How *did* they get started?

I bet the first time you picked up a newspaper it was like tuning into a soap opera when it was already twenty years into the story. Who are these people? And what's got them so excited? Where's Pine Valley? What happened to Tanzania? Now, which Canadian provinces speak French and which speak English?

Eventually we begin to pick out frequently repeated names in the news. And then they become familiar. And then we're off and running. Well, maybe off and walking.

As children we think that maybe when we get older we'll be able to understand the front page. But then we run out of time to follow it. Between breakfast, shaving, pulling on our stockings, delivering the kids, and catching the car pool, who has the chance to make a meaningful try at understanding the morning news? The traffic report is just about the extent of our early morning current events.

But reading the newspaper is your quick ticket to a more elevated standing in your company. Read the paper every day and you'll gradually build up your knowledge bank, which will position you for more respect and a higher income. You'll start noticing interesting connections between people or companies. And you'll start generating money-making and career-building ideas for you and your employer. I'll show you how later in this chapter.

For now I just want you to get used to the idea of reading the newspaper every day. And I've worked out an easy, time-efficient formula to help you use your daily newspaper to boost your standing at work. Right away.

GEORGE-ANNE'S 25-30-1 RULE

25

As in cents. Okay, maybe your daily newspaper is a little more expensive. But since the most important paper in my area is only a quarter, I've named the first part of this rule 25. Certainly, you can save money if you subscribe for home or office delivery. But if you're not yet in the habit of reading the newspaper, that's just another big investment to feel guilty about when the papers stack up unread. So just take it a day at a time, and fish out that quarter (or 35 cents or 50 cents) for your daily news.

30

Surely you can find thirty minutes somewhere in the day to read the newspaper. I know it sounds crazy. But remember, author Mary Higgins Clark began her multimillion-dollar mystery writing career as a struggling young widow with five children. She got up a couple of hours earlier than she had to to write a few pages before the children woke up. Hour by hour, page by page, she was building a future that brought her wealth beyond her wildest dreams. And *she* had to write. All I'm asking you to do is read! Which is a whole lot easier than writing, I assure you.

Now I could spend a whole day leisurely reading the newspaper—if I had the time. But if I waited until I had a whole day to read, I'd never read the newspaper! So by carving out only thirty minutes, you'll have a doable amount of time that will allow you to scan the headlines, note important names and details, and carefully consider one or two lengthy articles. Just be sure to find that thirty-minute time slot when you know you won't be interrupted. Read before the kids get up. Open up the paper on the subway (although, I personally find that really hard to do on crowded train cars), or, best yet, get to work a half hour early. That way, you'll read uninterrupted, and you'll start building your reputation as a thoughtful employee who is "in the know." (You'll also be near the rest room, so you can wash off that newsprint ink before it gets all over your clothes.)

1

Carefully and thoroughly read at least one article that's about a topic you are totally unfamiliar with or expect would be uninteresting. I'm not promising that every day will be a pleasant surprise when you do this. But as you build familiarity with a wide variety of the world's topics and issues, you'll be able to make creative connections that could change your life in an instant. Consider this habit your discovery adventure.

How to Read the Newspaper

If you're unaccustomed to studying the daily newspaper, go easy on yourself. Open the fun sections first: the sports section, the style section, the comics, or Ann Landers. But don't let anyone in your office see you read those sections. They're generally considered frivolous (although everyone reads them, when you get right down to it). And for heaven's sakes, don't clip and post the latest pertinent *Dilbert* or *Cathy* comic strips. I like them as much as the next person, but their humor shines a poor light on the workplace. Going public about how appropriate you find those strips positions you as cynical and dissatisfied on the job. *That* won't get you ahead.

Even when you're reading the fun sections, watch for important references and names. What socialite or sports team owner also owns a company that is somehow related to yours, either as a competitor, customer, or vendor? Make note of what these folks are doing and what they're personally interested in. It could come in handy one day.

Next, read the local section of the news. Remember, success comes when you're willing to do something that no one else wants to do. And, frankly, many people are tempted to skip the local section, because somehow local news just isn't as "important" or "serious" as national and international news. Scan the headlines for important connections to your company, business, supervisor, team members, or even yourself. These could be business leads. These could be job leads. Or they could be little tidbits that relate to a hobby that one of your colleagues enjoys. A clipping that says "I thought of you when I read this" may be just the thing to prompt your colleague to think of *you* the next time an interesting project comes along.

Next, read the national and international news. These articles will give you a solid idea of world trends, and a working vocabulary of important subjects for discussion in the boardroom, in the restroom, at the gym, or on the golf course. Don't worry, there will be no pop quiz at the end of the day, like those dreadful current events tests in school. So take your time getting to know the major players around the globe and what they stand for. Before long you'll know who's who, and you'll be caught up on this soap opera of world events.

Finally, spend at least the last ten minutes with the business section. For now, don't worry about all those stock exchange listings (unless you want to be active in the stock market). You can concentrate on the first few pages of the business section and gather up all sorts of information that will (not "could," *will*) make a difference in your career. This is where you will read interesting features on new companies in your community, legal trends that affect your workday, who got hired where, who got promoted, who has resigned to "pursue other interests." Most days it will seem as though none of this has any obvious meaning to you. But stick with it; eventually the big picture will sharpen in your mind and you'll begin to make connections and develop ideas that will benefit your own bank account.

What to Do With What You've Read

1. *Keep a personal clipping file.* This is another reason why the subway isn't the best place to read the paper. You're going to want plenty of room to tear it up and a neat place to stash the clippings. Read the paper with highlighter, scissors, and stapler within easy reach. Clip every article that appeals to you in even the slightest way. Circle important names and organizations that are quoted as experts in the article. Don't try to make sense of the reasons why you're interested. For now, just clip and save. Some lazy Sunday afternoon, you can pull out that file and leaf through the articles. Interesting patterns will reveal themselves: a frequently quoted person; a volunteer opportunity; an interest that might lead you to a more exciting place to work. Any one of these articles you've saved, or several considered together, could send you a bolt of inspiration that will send you along an exciting path of opportunity and new contacts.

2. *Clip articles that might be useful to a colleague.* Maybe there's a company mentioned that would be the perfect place for a team member to work or just to call to find further information to help get his or her job done. Or maybe another friend is considering accepting a job offer with a company that has just been publicized in connection with a discrimination lawsuit. Your friend will be forever grateful for that advance warning.

3. *Assemble your own personal list of names, organizations, and their contact information* (phone numbers, addresses, E-mail, etc.). Writers learn early in their careers that it's not as important to know all the answers as it is to know whom to call to get the answer when it's needed. That database will become increasingly valuable to you as you become known in your organization as the person who knows exactly

which person in what company has the answer to that million-dollar question.

4. *Create your own internal newsletter for distribution to your team or even throughout the company.* You may have seen professionally published newsletters circulated around the company. And you've probably noticed that they don't have to be fancy. In fact, the plainer they are, with just straight typing and simple layout, the more expensive they seem to be. Executives are willing to pay as much as $1,000 a year to subscribe to them because they don't have time to read the newspapers in search of those small details that relate only to their company, industry, or profession. Since you're already reading the newspaper every day, you've got the advantage.

Assemble all the meaningful details of the day, week, or month and distribute them throughout the company. Be sure to put your name prominently on the document, and you'll position yourself as both a valuable self-starter and someone with thoughtful judgment and meaningful background knowledge. Be sure to rewrite each news item in your own words and cite the reference so the reader can find the original article. And include a very short description of the news and why *you* think it's relevant to the company's interests.

Soon, you'll find managers and executives asking for your opinion. This is one project you can generate without asking for permission. And it's one project you can and should put your name on.

ADVANCED READING

When you're ready to broaden your exposure to business and culture trends, these are the publications you can gradually add to your list:

- *The Wall Street Journal*
- *The New York Times*
- *Newsweek, Time, U.S. News & World Report*
- *Fortune* magazine

- *Forbes* magazine
- *Fast Company* (this is especially important if your company is either a small start-up or a high-tech firm)
- The leading trade publication in your industry

A final note: As you add these publications to your reading list, make it obvious. Keep them on your desk if you can. Use your office address if you plan to subscribe to them (and if you can trust that they won't be lifted between the mail room and your desk). Offer to share your copies with others up and down the hierarchy in your office. Tuck in little notes to individuals, calling their attention to articles of specific interest.

And be sure to include on the route slip clear instructions to return the publications to their rightful owner. You!

It's said that knowledge is power. If a quarter can buy power, that's the best deal in town.

25

THE LANGUAGE OF SUCCESS

You probably recall the opening scene of *My Fair Lady* in which Henry Higgins rails on and on about "Why can't the English teach their children how to speak?" The way an Englishman speaks, he says, "absolutely classifies him." The way he says things "makes some other Englishman despise him."

That's all very amusing. Partly because you know it's true. The next time you ride on a crowded bus or take a plane somewhere tune your ears to the "eavesdrop channel" and see how many different accents you can pick up. You'll find yourself not only noticing the differences but also coming to conclusions about these people, such as where they're from or how well they're educated, just by listening to them speak. And you don't even have to look at them to know who you might like to get to know, and who is, well let's be honest, different from you.

There's a television commercial for a local car dealership that just drives me nuts in this way. In the opening scene, you can hear a ringing telephone and an unseen receptionist identifies the company and then says, "No. They're at the diner."

That's it. That's all she has to say to this customer who might have had the price of a car all in fresh bills stuffed into his pocket. In the next scene, the sales staff is crammed into a booth discussing sales strategies. Too bad for them the receptionist just rudely dismissed the one customer who might have taken that Rolls Royce off their hands.

Big deal. I'm still back with the receptionist, wanting to somehow train her to say instead, "They're all in a customer-service meeting at the moment. As soon as it finishes I'll have our manager call you immediately. May I have your number?"

And I can also tell you this: I have no idea which car dealership that is. I'm so freshly taken aback by the receptionist's uncultivated demeanor that the rest of the expensively produced commercial is lost on me.

So, what message is lost every time you open your mouth to speak? For that matter, what does your supervisor say that gives away his or her true feelings about the value of your work within the organization?

For instance, a couple of days ago I was reading Harvey Mackay's book *Beware the Naked Man Who Offers You His Shirt.* This book is full of wonderful ways to take a fresh look at your career. One chapter was entitled "You Only Get One Chance to Make a Good First Impression, and Yours is in the Hands of Your Receptionist."

Which is true. And I was very happy to see that he had included that bit of wisdom in this savvy little book. And, of course, since I agreed with him, I read the entire chapter. And I was horrified! The first sentence of the second paragraph reads, "Dead-end jobs are the toughest jobs in the world."

What? Is that how he really feels about his receptionist? That he or she (let's face it, probably a she) is in a dead-end job?

And then I thought, how did she feel when she read that her boss thinks she's in a dead-end job? And if she agrees with him, what kind of respect can she expect to receive from him.

A very bad sign indeed.

It's said that loose lips sink ships. I'd like to add to that "one word can kill a career." No, it doesn't rhyme, but it's more pertinent to our time.

As much as I would love to spend some time talking about grammar, that's not something a book like this can teach you. But here's a hint: Learn about double negatives, and the difference between "me" and "I." Get those down and you've positioned yourself for a raise.

Also, I would like to sensitize your ear to a few career sinkers.

- *"Just."* Are you just a secretary? I sure hope not. Employees in administrative support are working harder than anyone else up the corporate ladder. Your position is vital to getting the job done, or your company wouldn't be paying good money to keep that position filled.
- *"Stuff."* Turkeys are filled with stuff. Sausages are filled with stuff. Pillows are filled with stuff. Comedian George Carlin says that's what you need your house for, to keep all your stuff while you go out and get more stuff. But at work, there is no stuff. No one dreams big dreams and spends big money for stuff. At work you have "projects," "materials," "proposals," "equipment," "reports," and "product."
- *First names.* Your work environment is probably very casual and on a first-name basis. But if you are identifying yourself on the phone by just your first name, I want you to stop it right now. Your team members probably answer their phones with both their first and last names. Doesn't that sound respect-commanding? You deserve the same respect. Last names have historically been extremely important. People have died in duels because someone suggested someone else didn't have a last name. Now, we don't take ourselves quite that seriously anymore, but it's still ingrained in our subconscious that people who respect themselves enough to use their last name expect others to respect them equally.
- *Last names.* The flip side to this argument is the use of the last name. If your boss calls you by your first name but insists on being called by his or her last name, it's time to start looking for a new position. There is a fundamental disconnect between his or her idea of your prospects and your idea of self-worth. You don't have to take a new job right away, but knowing you're in demand will at least help neutralize that disrespect you must endure.

Always use last names when you're addressing a new visitor or an unfamiliar caller. That courtesy says to outsiders:

"We take our business and our business relationships very seriously. You are dealing with a world-class firm."

That little bit of formality might sound cold to you at first. You can balance that effect with a warm voice and personality, if you feel you need to. And in time you'll see that it actually projects your own self-respect. Surely people who do business with you would expect nothing less.

- *"With," "at," "for."* These are three prepositions that could be holding you back. Likewise, they could reveal volumes about what others really expect from you.

Tom, a self-employed friend of mine, was in the market for some office space a couple of years ago. Jane, an acquaintance in a related field, approached him with the idea of sharing a large space and joining forces when appropriate projects came their way. "Sounds reasonable," he thought. The space was larger and nicer than anything either of them could afford alone. So he explored the possibility. But then Jane ruined her plans by letting one word slip, the word "for." She was describing how she envisioned the two of them working, separately and together. And then she said that sometimes her projects would require heroic hours, adding, "Anybody working for me should expect to pull some late nights now and then." Oops. A split second later, all that was left of Tom was the fading warmth left in his empty chair.

There are times in your career when it makes sense to work *for* someone. When you are an apprentice and it's really an honor to be associated with such a master or leader. I don't think anyone would have any objection to working *for* Picasso or the President of the United States. (Sometimes a little humble pie now will get you places later.)

But, in truth, the only person you're working for is yourself—no matter who signs that paycheck. This has always been true, but it's even more obvious in today's environment of work teams. You don't work for a man or a woman. You work *for* you and *with* them.

And when someone asks you where you work, you don't work for IBM. That just screams servitude, doesn't it? No, you work *at* IBM. Two little letters. One little word. But it makes all the difference in your personal positioning.

Start seeing yourself as a peer of everyone you work with. Start conducting yourself with that level of confidence, more confidence probably than you might actually have at the moment. Pretty soon, you'll get used to that great feeling of respect.

- *"Girl."* Who's a girl? Certainly no one old enough to earn their own way. Now there are some regions in this country where "girl" is a harmless reference to a female person of any age. Although it still sets my teeth on edge. But then again, I live just down the road from Baltimore, where everyone is "Hon." So I had to learn to lighten up quick. My advice to you is pick your fights carefully. Use the word "woman" if you feel strongly about it, and hope that others will pick up the hint.

But there's another use for the word "girl" that I think is inexcusable. As in "I'll have my girl call your girl." I'm appalled that we still have to deal with that today. But, in some places we do. If you like your work in every other aspect, here's a way to put an end to that hideous expression. Try this approach: "Bob, it would be helpful if you used my name so Jane will know who will be calling her."

I know you probably would far prefer grabbing Bob by the neck and screaming, "Don't call me girl!" But that would be painting him into a corner, making him wrong, and leaving him no chance to recover his own dignity and make things right with you. That's a tough bit of wisdom for me to remember, as well. Sometimes being right feels more important than being effective. But there's a high price you will pay when you really need Bob on your side for a much more important issue down the road.

It's quicker to be direct and sharp. But consider these more gentle corrections part of your overall job description as facilitator. Efficiency is your responsibility, and if you couch your correction as a way you can help your team member be more efficient, your suggestion will be heard.

Try a phrase like "It will be helpful if . . ." It will take a little longer, but it will be worth it for both of you.

And maybe Harvey Mackay will read this chapter so I can tell him, "It would be helpful if you didn't call your receptionist's position a dead-end job. Because then you'd be able to attract dynamic representatives who would be very happy to put their best foot forward and be your first impression!"

———— PROFILE ————

Hannelore Uhl
Office Manager and Assistant to the President and CEO
Swissotel
New York, NY

I started out wanting to be a stewardess. I was a terrible student and detested school. I was born in 1947 in Germany, where there were few options for women in my generation. So secretarial training made sense. But so did traveling, so when I was eighteen I came to the United States as an au pair. And I discovered I liked New York very much.

I was, of course, fluent in German and English. I had a smattering of Italian and reading ability in French. There has always been a big demand for multilingual secretaries, which meant a big difference in pay. The first position I had was as a secretary in a pool. But within a year I worked my way out of the pool to become secretary to the president. That wasn't as big an achievement as it sounds, though. He was so difficult to work with that he couldn't hold on to secretaries. So eventually it was just a matter of my number coming up.

He would just scream out of his office for whatever he needed. It was very nerve-wracking. The day I quit was the day he hollered for the "red book," completely frustrated that I didn't have any idea what he was talking about. The red book! The red book! What he actually wanted was the Yellow Pages! It was hard to work with him, but having the experience of working for a president looked good on my résumé.

I can work and deal with people extremely well. But when they're abusive or extremely unfair, it will become evident that soon they won't appreciate the value and input you bring to the office. And it's time to start looking around. Bail out as quickly as you can.

I've been out of work three times in my life. I would sometimes make ends meet by working as a temporary. But that's really not my personality style. I'm a creature of habit, and going to a new office every couple of days or so and learning new processes are very unsettling for me.

Now, even though I'm a secretary myself, I also have four others reporting to me. I think I'm a good supervisor. I try to be fair and task-oriented. It's funny, though. I have such a commanding personality that people tend to come to me with their problems and issues. There's something about the way I project that makes people think I've got authority.

The boss I have now is brilliant. He's a true visionary. This company is growing immensely under his leadership, and I feel very privileged to have a closeup view of the future as he sees it.

My advice:

1. *Never stop educating yourself.* Keep current on both computer skills and the fields related to your business.

2. *Remember to stay flexible.* Be willing to adapt and roll with changes as they present themselves.

3. *Stay in related industries instead of jumping around all over the place.* It's much easier to understand what the business is all about, move up, and grab opportunities that present themselves because you're already on the information grapevine.

4. *Search for a position as high up the organizational hierarchy as possible.* When I call from this office I get done what I need to get done.

—————— 26 ——————

Secretary's Day . . .
Who Needs It?

The tradition of Secretary's Day takes quite a beating. And I think for good reason. It usually comes with flowers and a lunch date with the boss. That's just one thing the boss has to remember—and feel guilty about when he or she overlooks it. It carries the same kind of emotional and interpersonal political baggage that anniversaries and birthdays carry at home.

I find the celebration of Secretary's Day profoundly unprofessional. You don't celebrate Doctor's Day, Attorney's Day, or CFO Day. Observing Secretary's Day sets your function apart from the rest of the team's. And the custom of flowers and a meal is the custom of courtship, not a business relationship.

So you might be saying, "But I love Secretary's Day! The administrative staff in my company look forward to it every year. For us it's a festive occasion."

Well, I'm certainly not one to spoil the fun, but how about if I add to it instead? Take control of your company's Secretary's Day and turn it into an event driven by the administrative staff themselves!

Make Secretary's Day a company-wide project, with you as its CEO! Make Secretary's Day a blue ink day! Use this occasion to demonstrate your organizational skills, your leadership abilities, your creativity, and your talents for motivating and delegating to others.

Sound interesting? This is my idea, and as I'm writing this it's never been done before in any company. Let's make Secretary's Day the day the administrative profession takes over and shows corporate America the glory of its collective strength!

Let's turn Secretary's Day into a day of volunteerism for your colleagues! Here's what you do:

1. Soon after the winter holidays are over, say the end of January, start talking up the idea to your team, your department, your division, and your administrative peers. See which group would be most likely to get involved. Make this a casual conversation, nothing formal, nothing to make anybody nervous. And certainly don't ask your supervisor for permission. Children ask for permission. Businesspeople seek sponsorship, support, and endorsement. The time for that will come later.

2. Once you have your group of participants defined and assembled, start brainstorming ideas for a community event. Here are some ideas to get you started:

- Donate your corporate auditorium for a fund-raising concert to support your local orchestra.
- Work with your local Salvation Army to create a Secretary's Day version of its famous Angel Tree. Instead of a tree, set up a large boxwood bush, and hang paper roses from its branches. With each rose comes the name of a needy child and a list of needed spring clothes or summer toys.
- Coordinate with your local Christmas in April group and organize a team to spruce up someone's house.
- Paint a school.
- Hold an auction to raise funds for Operation Smile, your local women's shelter, or to support a veterinary clinic for pets from poor families.

These are just a few ideas. There are hundreds of charitable organizations that would love to hear from you and give you more advice on how to leverage all this volunteer energy you've stirred up.

3. Check with your community relations office to make sure that your project doesn't conflict with the corporate charity initiatives that they are tasked to manage.

4. Once you've decided on the charity for the year, plan down to the smallest possible detail and write a short proposal. Now is the time to approach your supervisor. Remember, you're not asking for permission. In fact you're offering to give your boss a break this year, all the while making him or her look good in the process. Your conversation should go something like this:

> Boss, I really appreciate the gestures you've extended to me over the years on Secretary's Day. But they are entirely unnecessary because I get a lot of satisfaction meeting and exceeding the goals we set every year. But this year I have another idea for how we can observe Secretary's Day, which gives back to the community. I've taken the liberty of brainstorming it with *x, x,* and *x.* And we've identified a one-day project we'd like to undertake instead. Here's the proposal. You'll see the expenses are nominal, but will provide priceless returns in internal and external goodwill. If you will consider endorsing it, the group can go ahead and take it from there.

5. Coordinate the event with your public relations office. This is good news about your company that they will want to publicize in the mass media.

6. Plan some kind of climactic event at the end of the day; something that your boss or CEO can come in on, where he or she can smile broadly for the camera and hand over a big check to the group you picked to support.

7. Let the bosses take credit externally for running the event. When the newspaper wants a quote, pass that opportunity up the ranks. But *you* take credit internally. You do this by thanking everyone. Send each participant a small token of thanks—try to make it as personal as you can. And it doesn't

have to be expensive. And, just as importantly, write two let-ters of thanks on internal letterhead. Send one to your boss, with a copy for the CEO. And send the other to your CEO, with a copy for the boss. Attach a report to each letter, outlin-ing exactly what was accomplished, what positive things exter-nal groups said about the company, and how much money was raised or saved. Keep a copy for your own files.

And don't forget to include it in your task log! This event will be a point of discussion during your next performance appraisal or salary review.

There are two more things you need to do before you close out Secretary's Day for the year:

8. Send a letter to your charity of choice, thanking them for the opportunity to participate in such an uplifting project. Additionally, start to develop relationships with all the other community charities. If your company has a community rela-tions department, that's normally their job. So ask them for advice on how you can continue this project without stepping on their toes.

9. Tell me all about it! Write me a letter describing the event, how it worked, and how it made you feel to give from such a well of abundance. It's a feeling that beats the heck out of a luncheon salad and a rose!

27

So How Did You Do This Year?

There used to be an old-fashioned rule of thumb for the appropriateness of well-bred women appearing in the newspaper. The proper woman is mentioned in the paper only three times in her life: when she's born, when she gets married, and when she dies.

Today this rule of three still applies in business to both men and women. There are three occasions in an individual's relationship with his or her employer when a future is decided: during the job interview, during the annual performance appraisal, and during the exit interview. We've already covered the job interview process. Let's take a look at the performance appraisal and the exit interview. How you handle them can affect your job today, and your standing with the company several years from now, even though you might be packing up your desk.

The Performance Appraisal

Here's a secret that you can make work for you: Most bosses hate performance appraisals. Performance appraisals typically mean annual performance *criticism*. To a supervisor, the process is a minefield of potential confrontations, emotional upset, and the possible loss of a valued employee. If he or she says the wrong thing to you in just the wrong way, you might up and quit!

Is there any wonder why performance appraisals keep getting put off, or why you have to pursue your supervisor to even put it on the schedule? And how suddenly the appraisal is bumped in favor of a more pressing demand for the supervisor's time?

Maybe you're breathing a sigh of relief. But don't. You're not doing yourself a favor by letting that annual meeting slide by, because it's usually during this process that your salary increase is discussed. And the longer you will have to live with your current income . . . when you deserve so much more. And, like putting off going to the dentist, putting off going through your annual appraisal isn't going to make the process any easier by the time you do it.

Here's what will make it easier: Grab this chance to reframe this dreadful event as yet another opportunity to market yourself as your supervisor's partner. Recast in both your minds the performance appraisal as a year-end status report between two partners.

In truth, the performance appraisal really is just a discussion to see how the company's objectives have been achieved over the last twelve months by your department. It's not a court of inquiry to establish your worthiness as a human being and your right to be on this planet. Your boss isn't going to point a laser gun to your head and blast you into the next galaxy. And you're not going to do that either.

Remember how I said earlier that part of what you're being paid to do is contain the panic quotient in the office? Here's a really good chance to shine and show your supervisor how incredibly businesslike and task-oriented you are. Take charge of your own performance appraisal!

Three weeks in advance of your anniversary (or whenever the appraisal would be scheduled), deliver a folder to your supervisor with these words:

"I see our annual performance review is coming up soon. I've scheduled it for thus and such date, if that's a good time for you. Here's a package of relevant materials I've put together to help you."

To help your boss in your own performance review . . . Wow, doesn't that sound cooperative?
This folder should include these items:

• *Three to five sheets from your task log over the past year that describe how you really reached way down to your toes to get your supervisor what was needed.* Don't just include day-to-day tasks; they're boring and they're what you're already being paid to do. What you want to do is demonstrate what you're doing that deserves an *increase.*

• *An updated job description.* If you've been on the job longer than three months you probably have outgrown the original job description. Things are happening that fast in corporate America. Let your supervisor know what your department really is doing.

• *A list of professional development initiatives you've assumed.* Have you taken classes at the local community college? Put it down. Have you finally gotten your college degree? Put it down. Have you taken German courses in your car on the way to work in the morning? Put it down.

• *You might also include a list of business-related books you've read over the year.* This may sound silly and remind you of your school's summer reading list. But some employers actually pay their employees to read, placing a dollar value on each title. Clearly, self-development is highly prized in all organizations. So use it to your advantage.

What you don't want to include is a list of gripes or excuses. I think those should be handled one-on-one in the review session. As modern and proactive as we want to be, the truth is, you're still the one being reviewed. Your review many not have the positive spin you might want it to have. You could get attacked in the review. And people have agendas that may have nothing to do with you, except that it suits their plans to have you gone. There's nothing like having in writing evidence of something that can be construed as your bad attitude. Negative comments can be taken out of context, and the next thing you know you're being disciplined for insubordination.

Writing is permanent. So only put in writing what represents you in a positive light.

If you need to calm your nerves, repeat to yourself over again: This is a year-end partnership meeting. The two of you are discussing the state of the department, much as the President of the United States discusses the State of the Union. The two of you are on the same side, the same team. Establish that convivial tone now, and your relieved supervisor will be more than happy to follow your leadership in this meeting.

It's a personal marketing issue. You're establishing how your presence translates into profitability for the company. *You are your own best cost-benefit analysis.*

In truth, performance appraisals shouldn't be done once a year. Feedback should be given constantly. If your boss isn't big on feedback, develop your own system of getting it anyway. Solicit it. Which might be hard to do, because your boss is being paid to make money for the company, not hold your hand and cultivate your career. So you have to ask for feedback in such a way that it's obvious to your boss that it's to his or her advantage to guide you along.

Request your feedback in a context in which your boss will see a direct benefit. Always point to what's in it for him or her.

Your boss says, "What's important to me is a smoothly running ship." Then you say, "Regular feedback will help me refine my systems and run the ship better."

At the end of the meeting, always talk about establishing goals and objectives for both the department and your own professional development. That's not out of line. Corporations invest millions in bringing along their management staff.

You and your profession deserve the same considerations. You're not being overlooked because corporations don't think you're worth bringing along (well, sometimes that's the case). Generally you're being overlooked because corporations aren't used to thinking about the office support profession at all. They're still operating under the old paradigm that the higher the salary, the higher the return on investment for developing that individual's career. But in truth, you are so valuable that you probably are going to outlast most middle and upper-middle managers. So companies need to recognize that you represent a long-term investment for them.

What happens when your current boss does leave? Initiate a performance review with your new boss immediately. Unless your company does team interviewing, in which you had a hand in interviewing and selecting your department's new supervisor, the chances are good that you'll be meeting this person after the deal is sealed. It's worse than an arranged marriage. What are the chances the chemistry will work?

Improve your odds by being the one to set the meeting. Most of us would never dare to do that because it would seem too presumptuous. But it's not. You are doing your new supervisor a service by orienting this person to the department from your perspective. Describe to this new hire what your functions have been during the past year, and how reality has compared with the formal job description.

Don't rely on your outgoing boss to adequately introduce his or her replacement to the workings of your department and your position. You would be putting your career second to other people's priorities. And we know where that will lead you. Nowhere. The outgoing supervisor has his or her mind focused on the new job. You're history to that person. But you're not history to yourself. You are your own future. So step up and speak up.

Starting out on the right foot together is in everyone's best interest. And this initial interview is your chance to size up this new hire. If he or she treats you like "just a secretary," this is your chance to find out before it's too late. And start looking for a new position yourself.

THE EXIT INTERVIEW

So now you have found a much better place to work. Your new boss treats you like the seasoned professional that you are. You have a better salary, and the company pays your tuition.

But first you have to go through one more dog-and-pony show at your soon-to-be former employer: the exit interview. I don't think the personnel staff who administer the interview are really clear what these interviews are for. The exit interviews I've witnessed consist of boring, droning, endless questions to get irrelevant details. And all the while you just want to get out of there!

Typically, they really don't want to know that your boss has been a pain in the neck and has treated you disrespectfully, and that you've found greener pastures elsewhere.

So, once again, use the interview to your advantage. Solidify your relationship within the company by being gracious, informative, and respectful of the supervisor you are leaving. Just because you're quitting the company it doesn't mean your relationship with the organization is over. It's possible you're going to meet these people in business circles for the rest of your life. You want to cultivate a residual reputation, one that spreads your name through the grapevine when recruiters are looking for someone just like you for that next better paying position. You want great recommendations for the future. And it's possible you want a door to remain open at the company you're leaving. A lot of people leave an organization, only to come back at a huge salary increase.

But, if you get one of those sing-song "I have to fill out this form" drones putting you through an inquisition, just put up your hand to say "Stop." Tell this individual, "It's been a pleasant experience working here, but I'd rather not spend my time doing it this way."

What are they going to do if you don't play along, fire you?

Always leave your direct supervisor on the best of possible terms. You will see that person again. One young woman I know started her career working in a very small company run by an alcoholic. In the morning his desk drawer would be filled with new beer cans. By the afternoon it would be filled with empty ones. She couldn't wait to get out of there!

A friend saw her potential and recruited her to join a much larger organization. She was so happy to have a new future! But, fortunately for her, she kept her cool at the first company. Because, lo and behold, she wasn't at the new job more than two weeks—two weeks!—when a memo arrived on her desk announcing the appointment of a new senior executive. Guess who? Neither of them had known the other was interviewing at the same organization. But she had left the first company gracefully. And this man stayed out of her way in the new company.

Always leave gracefully. Leave people with a positive impression about you. Leave 'em laughing. If you're leaving under any sort of cloud, emotional or otherwise, remember to take the high road out.

28

HOW TO KNOW WHEN TO GO

As we've already said, the old traditional job contract is dead. Just because you do excellent work, have perfect attendance, and are a high producer doesn't mean you are guaranteed a job for life. Employers are now telling you to continue to contribute to the organization's goals and objectives, continue to keep your skills current (even cutting edge), and find new ways to add value to your position; and maybe, just maybe, there will be a role for you this week and maybe even next month. But don't expect much more than that.

Okay, fair enough. Now you know the ground rules. You know you must maintain a clear vision of who you are in the workplace and what skills and energies you bring to your current organization's bottom line. But shouldn't there be something in return? Isn't that part of the New Deal? Corporations were supposed to have started saying, "Stop expecting us to behave like parents, and we'll start treating you like adults."

It seems that as far as many organizations are concerned, the New Deal means they will relinquish any long-term obligation for your security. But in exchange . . . nothing. A report published in late 1997 by the international management consulting firm Towers Perrin reflected that employers are looking for high performance and they recognize that employees are a tremendously important resource. But they haven't made any changes to support their own performance-oriented management change. The *1997 Workplace Index* showed that:

- Employees are increasingly doubtful that management considers their interests in decisions that affect them.
- Employees are less convinced their managers and supervisors are helping them develop, learn, and grow.
- Employees don't see any links among performance, pay, and developing best-available talent. In short? Generally speaking, you're on your own. Even if you work for a company that's aggressive in training all employee levels, there's no guarantee that development philosophy won't be obliterated in the name of grabbing an edge in stock market prices. In fact, there's no guarantee you won't be asked to take a pay cut in the name of marketplace competitiveness.

"Hey!" they reason, "don't like it? You can always leave."

So that's the New Deal: Expect nothing but the freedom to hunt for a new job. Your obligation to yourself is to know exactly what you expect from your job (livelihood? money for a child's education? security? a growth future? self-esteem?). Know how to recognize whether you're getting it or not. And then have the system in place to find new work as soon you're ready to move on.

I can't tell you how to make these decisions for yourself because your set of circumstances is uniquely your own. For instance, I know one brilliant administrative assistant who is well-respected by her boss, who says he wants her to learn more about how the organization functions overall. And she sincerely wants to. But he excludes her from staff meetings and refuses to pay for outside tuition. He's afraid, she says, that she'll leave if she gets more knowledge and skill. Still, in her performance ratings he criticizes the fact that she shows no interest in developing herself.

That would drive me crazy! Frankly, it makes her nuts. But still she doesn't quit. Why? Because otherwise—and I stress *otherwise*—their relationship works for her. She's close to retirement, her salary is the household's second income, which is dedicated to paying tuition. The commute is less than fifteen minutes. The entire staff is like a big family, celebrating and supporting each other in major personal life events. And she and her boss are a well-tuned unit of partnership and efficiency. They know what to expect from one another, and he lets her do her work without disruptions. In short, she gets what she needs. And no one can know her well enough to advise her otherwise. Certainly not me.

Stay or go, the power is *yours* to make your own decisions. But I've seen some situations in which the abuse is so bad that the administrative assistants have lost all faith in their ability to captain their own lives and futures. So I'd like to run through some various warning stages that might signal that it's time to get your résumé in order and your contacts warmed up.

No Learning Support

You must constantly upgrade your skills and knowledge to merely keep up in today's marketplace. Your professional training should never stop. If your company does not support your development, this tells me two things that aren't very hopeful about your prospects there.

First, any company that doesn't take pride in its employee education is ignorant of current management trends, is undervaluing the importance of its employees, and has lost its competitive edge. Second, if the company's training programs are available only to senior and management staff—and not support staff—you're working for a dope who doesn't respect you.

You won't grow under these circumstances. With today's developing technology and rapidly changing marketplace, you must stay on top of trends. Find a company that respects that, and you've found your next step to the future.

High Turnover All Around You

If you're new to an organization or department, and it seems as if everyone else is as well, the company might have just undergone a major re-engineering. That's a common scenario these days, but it does take a toll on the morale of the few surviving longtime employees. Or it's possible that your team supervisors can't hold on to assistants because they don't understand the value of the services you provide. Pay attention to the word on the grapevine; listen to it all, but take it with a little grain of salt. If you're new, you might not know who is legitimately disgruntled and who is merely attitude-impaired. Either way, the signs are discouraging. So keep that stack of résumés you made, and keep your motor running.

ILLEGAL/UNETHICAL REQUESTS

For almost every headline about an executive or company in dutch with the law, there is an administrative assistant who knew what was going on but kept his or her mouth shut. You may one day have a boss who asks you to pad an expense account, lie on a research report, shred a condemning document, fib to a spouse, or lie to a summons server. You know what your ethical boundaries are. Hold on to them, because it's *your* face you must look at first thing in the morning. You don't have to quit, but you can say no to an order that you know is wrong. And you won't have to do any explaining. Your boss knows it's wrong, too. And he or she probably wouldn't appreciate being preached to. But he or she also probably wouldn't appreciate being said no to either. You don't necessarily have to quit, and you don't necessarily have to go running to the department head or human resources. But it would be smart to keep a log of these requests. If you find yourself passed up for a promotion and pay raise and it looks like a retaliation move, march that log right down to HR.

COMPANY MISSION OR MANAGEMENT PHILOSOPHY

I could give you all sorts of examples of companies over the last several years that fell into public disfavor because of their management practices. But I don't want to tell you how to set up your own value system. This is an ethical consideration that only you can wrestle with on your behalf. Just remember that you spend most of your waking hours at work, and how you choose to invest that time says volumes about your character. Wouldn't you rather spend that time working for a company that makes the world a better place to live in?

ABUSIVE BOSSES

This is the one area in which I'm not going to give you any latitude for weighing pros and cons. There's no choice. If the way your supervisor treats you erodes your self-esteem or makes you doubt your capability and value to the organization, take action! Now!

There is so much in the newspapers and magazines about domestic violence but very little about that same kind of abuse in relationships at work. Spouses start abusing their mates in subtle ways, increasing and escalating the violence as the months and years go on. At home, the abuse might eventually turn to physical violence. That rarely happens in the workplace. It's too public, too obvious. But at work or at home, the issue remains the same, one of control. If the abusers can't control their spouses, they can certainly control their assistants. The power to control is built into the organizational hierarchy.

But for some supervisors, that amount of power isn't enough. And they have to build it up by tearing you down. I'm not talking about periodic moodiness here. This is serious, chronic behavior that will destroy your self-esteem before you even know it. If you find yourself working for a screamer, someone who throws things, someone who calls you names, someone who lies to you, someone who makes you think you're worthless, make moves to leave. *Do not tolerate it for a second longer.*

Take the time to go through company channels only if you have a long-term relationship with your employer (and built-up equity in a retirement program) or if you have faith in the company's overall commitment to a quality workplace environment.

But even if you're working with the official reporting

process, take your own career in your own hands. Get that résumé out. Respond to job opening announcements. Just that active role in regaining control of your life again will help neutralize your boss's abuse as you wait for your own events to unfold.

I can't promise you that you'll land another job right away, but I can promise you this: The longer you take to leave, the harder it will be to leave. Your boss will be increasingly successful in convincing you that you're worthless. You'll be too depressed and overwhelmed to confidently land job interviews. And you might even become victim of the Stockholm Syndrome, which psychologists discovered when they observed that kidnapping victims frequently transfer their sympathies to their own captors!

Once you start hearing yourself say, "But he's my boss and he needs me," grab yourself by your collar, if you have to, and haul yourself out of that company.

After you've been gone a month or more, get together with some of your friends from the old company. You might be amazed to discover that as you reclaimed your own life and career and left, they were all applauding and yelling, "Way to go!"

Where to Go?

Of course, for most of us the ideal way to part company with an employer is with a two-weeks notice. And that's only after we have leisurely conducted a job search that has netted us a more promising and interesting position, complete with a respectable salary increase. But sometimes it just doesn't work out that way. And we have to close our eyes, hold our nose, and take a big leap of faith.

No matter what the circumstances of your departure, there is at least one place to go—temporary help services. Now I recognize that times change, and certainly there are different job markets throughout the United States. But I will tell you that overall in the late 1990s, there was a huge demand for available talent of all levels and professions—even medical doctors among temporary help companies! The demand is getting even louder as national unemployment stays in the single digits and permanent companies are snapping up all available job candidates.

As a result, temporary help companies are becoming more lavish in the opportunities and benefits they offer the workers they send out on assignments—even offering health and retirement benefits.

The temporary help approach is a fabulous solution if you

- Are between jobs and need steady, regular income
- Are new to town and want to take your time getting to know the major employers by getting an inside look at their corporate culture
- Want to update and upgrade your skills
- Want to stay current in the marketplace but need more control over the hours and days you work

Here's a tip from a friend of mine who started her career as a temp in Washington, D.C.: Print your own business cards, complete with all your contact information (don't forget your E-mail address). Working as a temporary is a quick way to beef up your contact list. So, when you hit it off especially well with people you meet via temping, exchange cards with them. Get in touch now and then. Maybe one day they'll hear of a job that's perfect for you. And they'll know how to find you. (Or vice versa! Moving from office to office will give you lots of information on opportunities that you can share with your growing collections of contacts).

Just a little warning: Temporary help companies want to be sure that you won't return to their clients on a freelance basis. So keep in touch all you want with your new contacts. But if they want you back, be sure to let your temporary help company manage the assignment. That's how they stay in business.

29

WELL-DONE AND JUST BEGUN

This chapter marks the end for me but only the beginning for you. If I've done my job, you should now be inspired to boost your career to new levels of ambition, reward, and respect.

To be entirely fair, I must advise you to expect changes in your career right away. You are not the same person you were before you picked up this book. In fact, I'm not the same person I was when I started writing it. Just as I've been saying all along, projects are growth opportunities, full of pleasant challenges and worrisome obstacles. And writing this book has been the biggest challenge of my life. But not the last, I'm sure.

We've gone through a great deal of material together. There's so much to digest in such a small book. So I thought I'd leave you with a parting gift—a quick review of the main ideas. If you ever feel confused about your career's direction, return to this last chapter and consider these points. I hope they'll be enough to spark your memory and help you refocus your purpose.

1. *Believe in your company, and only work at a company that believes in you.* You alone are responsible for the way you choose to invest your working hours. And you alone must face your conscience in the morning. Make sure you feel confident that your company is somehow making this world a better place to live in.

2. *Remember that whatever you are willing to tolerate, you* will *be asked to tolerate.* Make allowances for other people's moodiness, yes, but accept nothing less than respectful, courteous treatment.

3. *Your task log will be your most important tool for graduating yourself to more interesting projects and custom designing your career.* Keep those yellow, blue, and green markers handy. Over a period of only three months, they will tell the real story of how you do your job.

4. *The bigger the project, the bigger the paycheck.* Your own value will increase accordingly.

5. *Success depends on the relationships you build.* Recruit sponsors within and outside your company. It's not as important to know all the answers as it is to know the people who have the answers.

6. *To get ahead, groom the person positioned to replace you.* Remember the Paula Principle: Your potential for success is limited only by your willingness to help the person coming up behind you be successful, too.

7. *Make sure your image supports your success.* Reconsider everything that surrounds you: your appearance, your workstation, even the casual social circles you run in at work. Just as outgrown shoes make you feel bad because they're too tight, outgrown habits have a way of making you uncomfortable, too.

8. *Treat others the way they want to be treated.* Get results by accommodating the personality styles of your team members.

9. *Knowledge is power.* Read the newspaper every day. Commit yourself to the 30-25-1 Rule.

10. *Change is good; control is better.* Change is also inevitable, so you're better off learning how to control your reaction to it.

11. *Avoid Yes Stress.* Choose and set your boundaries. Learn to say no without closing the door on future yeses.

12. *Learn the language of success.* Train yourself to speak correctly. Use your last name when you identify yourself. You work *with* a person and *at* a company. You work *for* yourself.

13. *Get what you need by using cost-benefit analyses.* They're easy to do, and they'll reap tangible rewards, as well as new respect for your businesslike approach.

How odd it feels to be wrapping up a project that's consumed my attention for so long. So, here's the last piece of advice I have for you. And I must apply it myself, as I turn off my computer in two seconds:

14. *Learn to recognize when your job is done and it's time to move on.*

MANAGING MULTIPLE BOSSES OR ONE BOSS WITH THE WORK TASK LOG

TIME?	CLIENT?	KIND?	DUE?	LONG?	INTERRUPT?	RESULT?